BALLPARKS

Previous page: Looking toward Fenway Park's diamond in the 1950s. The "Green Monster" is on the right.
National Baseball Hall of Fame

Above: Fireworks at Oakland Coliseum during the singing of national anthem on opening night in 1998.
San Francisco Chronicle

BALLPARKS

A Panoramic History

MARC SANDALOW & JIM SUTTON

CHARTWELL
BOOKS

This edition published in 2014 by

CHARTWELL BOOKS
an imprint of Book Sales
a division of Quarto Publishing Group USA Inc.
276 Fifth Avenue Suite 206
New York, New York 10001
USA

© 2014 by Greene Media Ltd.
34 Dean Street, Brighton, BN1 3EG

From an idea proposed by Frank Oppel

Design: Tony Stocks@Greene Media Ltd.

Photographs
All images are credited with their captions. Photos came from Getty Images, Corbis, the Baseball Hall of Fame, Digitalballparks.com, Roger Miller, and the San Francisco Chronicle: thanks to all those who helped.

ISBN-13: 978-0-7858-3174-7

Printed and bound in China

Dedicated to the late Jim Sutton

Right: Workmen from the Wrigley Field grounds crew shovel snow from the infield of the park on April 7, 2003. The Chicago Cubs were to play their home opener against the Montreal Expos but the game was cancelled due to the snow.
Getty Images

CONTENTS

INTRODUCTION

Baseball is unique among American sports. Football, basketball, and hockey are played on identical fields, courts, and rinks. Only in baseball does the park define the game.

There is simply no feeling like walking into a ballpark on an early spring day and taking in the expanse of lush, green, meticulously groomed, and mostly uninhabited grass. There is a buzz, a smell, and an excitement to a baseball stadium that cannot be recreated on the evening news or the morning's sports pages, as dutifully as they try.

The Green Monster in Boston, the ivy in Chicago, the center field hill in Houston, the Bermuda Triangle in Miami, the convertible roof in Seattle, and the cove in San Francisco: these not only brand each park with a distinct appearance, they change the way the game is played.

There is little discussion of how many baskets Wilt Chamberlain would have shot, or how many goals Wayne Gretsky would have scored, had they spent their careers at the Boston Garden. Yet baseball fans can spend hours debating what Babe Ruth might have done as a Fenway slugger; how many home runs Willie

Mays might have hit if not for the wind at Candlestick Park; or whether the Minnesota Twins would have won a world championship, let alone two, if not for the helpful horrors of their Metrodome. A game at Wrigley Field in Chicago is a very different experience than one at Dodger Stadium in Los Angeles, or Pro Player in Miami.

This book tries to highlight those differences. It is not an authoritative account of baseball stadiums, or a encyclopedic telling of their history. Instead, it is a picture-filled look at what makes the current major league parks, and some of the famous old ones, so special.

To anyone trying to write about ballparks, it is quickly apparent that parks are in a perpetual state of change. Since Baltimore Memorial Stadium opened in 1954, well over forty new ballparks have been constructed, several of which have already been replaced and demolished. As this book was olriginally being researched, two ballparks changed their names, and two others shut their doors to make way for new ones. By next season, many of the parks

described in this book will have undergone some renovations. To a baseball fan, the changes provide a fascinating glimpse at the game's evolution.

The quirkiness and intimacy of the turn-of-the-century ballparks was largely the product of geography and finances, as team owners tried to cram stadiums into small urban lots, in places where fans would be plentiful. If the lot was misshaped, as at Washington's Griffith Stadium (where one home owner refused to budge from the stadium site), the crooked outfield wall was simply built around it. Fenway's Green Monster was erected because of the park's tight quarters, and to block residents on Lansdowne Street from getting a free look at the game. Such quirks are now carefully added to stadium designs, sometimes at great additional cost, to capture a sense of history and tradition.

Today, it is also an article of faith among baseball owners that stadiums should be intimate and small, built to boost home run totals to lure fans to the games. Yet in 1910, when Charlie Comiskey built a park on the south side of Chicago for his White Sox, he wanted a

huge outfield, partly for the thrill of watching fielders make long sprints for balls, and for the excitement of watching runners try for extra base hits, rather than lope around the bases in a lazy home run trot.

A generation from now, the game will have evolved again. Perhaps the short fences that mark early 21st century parks will seem like dinosaurs. Just as the opening of steel-and-concrete Shibe Park in Philadelphia in 1909 and the opening of Oriole Park at Camden Yards in Baltimore in 1992 touched off revolutions in ballpark designs, it is easy to imagine some future innovation changing the look of baseball stadiums.

Some qualities seem certain to endure. The perfect diamond, the lush turf, the intimacy between the players and the fans, the geographic landmarks that let you know exactly where the game is being played. For 30 major league cities, there are few structures that better tell their story than their ballpark.

The historian Jacques Barzun famously wrote: "Whoever wants to know the heart and mind of America, had better learn baseball." In a similar

Fans are what it's all about. Will this new generation of Cubs' fans still be visiting Wrigley Field with their children? Victor Ireland, Jacob Peckerson, and Sinhue Mendoda show their loyalty to the Cubs before the game against the Florida Marlins, October 7, 2003.
Photo by Brian Bahr/Getty Images

vein, whoever wants to know baseball had better learn ballparks. This book is a start.

Acknowledgments

Everyone has an opinion about ballparks. Thanks to Vernard Atkins, Zac Coile, Bob Congdon, Bonnie DeSimone, Ed Epstein, Carl Nolte, Marcie Sandalow, and Ellen Loerke for sharing their insightful views with us. Special thanks to Tom McClurg for his careful reading of the text and his constant reminder of what makes baseball great.

Many people helped in the hunt for photos. Special thanks to W.C. Burdick of the National Baseball Hall of Fame, Marc Seigerman at Getty Images, Gary Fong at the *San Francisco Chronicle*, Tony Pastore of Digital Ballparks.com, Rob Arra of Everlasting Images, Roger Miller of Baltimore's Roger Miller Studio. Ltd., and to Sandra Forty.

Thank you, every one and all.

Jim Sutton, who died in late 2009, would have been directly involved in revising this new edition: an admirable researcher and publisher, he is sorely missed.

Exterior view of Camden Yards late in the afternoon of August 15, 2003, during the game between the Orioles and the Yankees. The Yankees won 6–4. This retro design influenced a new generation of ballparks designed for baseball rather than ground-sharing with football. The new Marlins Park is the first to throw off this approach for a more modern 21st century design.
Photo by Jerry Driendl/Getty Images

THE AMERICAN LEAGUE

The roster of American League cities sounds like a refrain from a Chuck Berry song: Detroit, Chicago, Baltimore, Boston, and K.C. When it was founded in 1901, the American League was the junior circuit, coming to life a quarter of a century after the National League, and bringing professional baseball to America's thriving metropolises. Of the eight original American League cities, all still have a professional team.

Some American League teams have come and gone, such as the Boston Pilgrims, the Cleveland Naps, the Seattle Pilots, and the Washington Senators. Some fifty stadiums have been home to American League teams. Several of the old classics—Detroit's Tiger Stadium, Cleveland's Municipal Stadium, and Chicago's Comiskey Park—closed in the 1990s.

The American League's oldest stadium is Fenway Park, which opened the same week the *Titanic* sank in 1912. Exactly 80 years later, Baltimore's Camden Yards sparked a new wave of classic-style parks, structures which sought to imitate the intimacy of Fenway and other older parks. The latest addition to the league, the Astros, boasts a modern (2000) ballpark.

There are now new ballparks in Minnesota, New York (two of them) and Washington. In Oakland, with the O.co Coliseum lease due to expire in 2015, the location of the A's future home is still as uncertain as it has been since talks started in the mid-2000s.

Fenway Park seen from inside the Boston Red Sox dugout during the game against the Yankees on July 25, 2003. The Yankees won 4–3.
Photo by Jerry Driendl/Getty Images

AMERICAN LEAGUE EAST

The major change to the ballparks of the American League's Eastern Division is the loss of one of the most storied parks in baseball—Yankee Stadium—leaving Fenway Park as the only old-ster. Fenway is where Babe Ruth began his career, and Yankee is where he reached power-hitting immortality. Ty Cobb, Walter Johnson, Hank Greenberg, Jimmy Foxx, Tris Speaker, each played on those very fields but only the Red Sox still play there. Fans can still sit in the same Boston bleachers where Ted Williams hit his longest shot, but no longer in Yankee Stadium where Lou Gehrig bid baseball adieu.

To the north, SkyDome—now the Rogers Centre—with its convertible roof, showed the sporting world how to handle the elements. Orioles Park at Camden Yard reminded fans of the game's intrinsic beauty, while Tropicana Field in Florida jammed about as much entertainment as can fit inside a structure built for baseball.

The refurbishment of Fenway Park means that the venerable centenarian meets 21st century standards. The other parks of the American League Eastern Division largely look like they are here to stay.

Right: Oriole Park at Camden Yards during the game between the Orioles and the Yankees on August 14, 2003. The Yankees won 4–3.

Photo by Jerry Driendl/Getty Images

BALTIMORE ORIOLES

ORIOLE PARK AT CAMDEN YARDS

BALTIMORE ORIOLES

Address:
333 West Camden Street
Baltimore, MD 21201
Capacity: 50,386
Opening day: April 6, 1992—Baltimore Orioles 2,
Cleveland Indians 0
Cost to construct: $110 million
Architect: HOK Sports
Dimensions (ft):
Left Field—333
Left Center—364
Center Field—410
Right Center—373
Right Field—318
Defining feature: B&O Warehouse in right field
Little-known ground rule: Fly ball hitting the
grounds crew shed roof in right field and bouncing back
into play: Home Run
World Series: None
All-Star Game: 1993

Memorable moments:
1993 July 13—Seattle's Ken Griffey Jr. becomes the first
    player to hit the B&O warehouse on a fly, during a
    home run contest preceding the All-Star game.
1995 September 6—Cal Ripken Jr. smacks a fourth-
    inning home run while playing in his 2131st con-
    secutive game, surpassing Lou Gehrig as baseball's
    "Iron Man."
1996 September 6—Eddie Murray hits his 500th home
    run.
2007 August 22—Orioles lose 30-3 to the Texas
    Rangers.
2012 September 13—By beating the Rays the Orioles
    reach their 81st victory of the season and go on
    to end their 14-year losing drought with a wild
    card berth against the Rangers. The Orioles win
    5-1 and play the Yankees for the ALDS.
2012 October 8—Victory for the Orioles over the
    Yankees, but they will come off worse overall 3-2.

The opening of Oriole Park at Camden Yards touched off a baseball revolution. After three decades of constructing cookie-cutter coliseums, Baltimore reintroduced the concept of a ballpark. Nestled beside train lines in the city's inner harbor, the yard was a throwback to the days of Babe Ruth, who had been born just two blocks away. Its brick facade, asymmetrical outfield, panoramic view of downtown Baltimore, and the imposing B&O warehouse—which taunts left handed hitters—reminded Americans why baseball was long regarded as the national pastime.

The rest of the baseball world took notice. Within a decade, ballparks in Cleveland, Denver, Pittsburgh, San Francisco, Arlington, Seattle, Atlanta, Milwaukee, Houston, Detroit, and San Diego would mimic Baltimore's old-time appeal.

Baseball history guided the architects, who were influenced by Ebbets Field (Brooklyn), Shibe Park (Philadelphia), Fenway Park (Boston), Crosley Field (Cincinnati), Forbes Field (Pittsburgh), Wrigley Field (Chicago), and the Polo Grounds (New York). The cozy dimensions, the steel trusses, the rustic clock on the center field scoreboard, all gave the park a classic feel.

But the park is new. It has luxury boxes (a major revenue source), microbrews, a family picnic area, and shiny bronze baseballs imbedded in Eutaw Street, which runs between the warehouse and the outfield bleachers. Just beyond the bleachers, fans can buy barbeque made by Oriole great Boog Powell, who can sometimes be found signing hot dog wrappers and ticket stubs.

The history is more than just appearance. Ruth's father owned a tavern about where center field now sits. The eight-story, red-bricked, turn of the century B&O warehouse, the park's defining feature, is more than 1,000 feet long, built in 1895 to handle long railroad freight cars, and is said to be the longest building on the East Coast. It sits 432 feet away from home plate and though Ken Griffey Jr. reached it during a home run competition before the 1993 All-Star Game, no one has yet done so during a game. The park's anchor in a revitalized downtown was a big reason that the legislature agreed to help pay for it with the sale of lottery tickets. When it was built, Maryland Governor William Donald Schaefer called the ballpark "the largest single economic development opportunity we have had in the last decade," and its success spurred other clubs to look beyond land-rich suburban areas for their stadium homes.

The move from Baltimore's old Memorial Stadium to Camden Yards "is like coming from the slums to a palace," Orioles' outfield David Segui said the week the park opened. "If we play half as good as this place looks we'll be pretty good this year."

Unfortunately for O's fans, the park has fared better than the Orioles who are still looking to bring a World Series to Camden Yards.

The Orioles have made a number of changes to the ballpark in recent years, with a new HD display after the 2008 season, major improvements to seating and skyboxes which reduced capacity to just under 46,000. Further changes in the 2011–12 off season improved sightlines from Eutaw street and added a lounge to the top of the batter's eye, increasing capacity to over 50,000.

Above: The south end of Eutaw Street enters Camden Yards and runs alongside the stadium's right field affording views of the field of play. In the 2011–2012 off season the right-field wall was lowered from 25 to 21 feet to improve the view. On game days, the entrance to Eutaw Street is ticketed and when seating is sold out, the street provides some standing room. The street itself is studded with small plaques identifying where home runs have landed. Here it is seen thronging with fans before a game.
Digitalballparks.com

Right: A sculpture of Babe Ruth stands tall outside Oriole Park at Camden Yards. George Herman "Babe" Ruth (1895–1948) was born in Baltimore but started his long career in 1914 with the Boston Red Sox. It was with the Yankees 1920–34 that he came to the fore with prodigious batting feats—54 home runs, then a record, in 1920; 60 in 1927. Among the greatest players baseball has ever seen, he played in 10 World Series, hit 714 home runs (a record that stood until 1974), and was elected to the Hall of Fame in 1936.
Photo by Jerry Driendl/Getty Images

Night panorama of Oriole Park.
Photo by Jerry Driendl/Getty
Images

Left and Above: Night falls over Baltimore and Oriole Park in this 2003 photograph, the out-of-town scoreboard lighting up in the fading light. Babe Ruth was born two blocks from the ballpark 75 years before Oriole Park opened in 1992. The long building past right field is a remnant from the days of the "B&O"—the Baltimore & Ohio Railroad. Built at the turn of the century the warehouse is 1,016 feet long and is used today to house the Orioles' management offices as well as restaurants and bars. Much of the success of the new park has been attributed to its location in the midst of Baltimore's bustling inner harbor.
Photos by Roger Miller

Right: Bleachers and scoreboard from right field: note the B&O warehouse at right and the Emerson Bromo-Seltzer Tower in the distance. Listed on the National Register of Historic Places, the Bromo-Seltzer Tower was modeled after the Palazzo Vecchio in Florence, Italy. It was completed in 1911 and has been a Baltimore landmark ever since. It was built by Captain Isaac Emerson, the inventor of Bromo-Seltzer.
Digitalballparks.com

Left: Pre-game introduction of the home team on April 6, 1992, the first home game of the season for the Orioles and the first official game played at Oriole Park at Camden Yards. A capacity crowd of more than 48,000 enjoyed a beautiful day at the new ballpark and a victory celebration as the Orioles beat the Cleveland Indians, 2–0.
Photo by Roger Miller

Right: The outside of Camden Yards with gate D right of center. The stadium had an electrifying effect on its neighborhood. Architects Populous say that "the year Oriole Park opened, downtown Baltimore spending increased 260 percent. More than 15 years after its opening, Oriole Park's presence was still making an impact; it continues to generate more than $165 million in sales and tax revenues near $10 million per year."
Digitalballparks.com

Left: Spectators outside Oriole Park's oldest feature, the B&O warehouse. From the high point of 1997 when attendance was over 3.7 million, the Orioles now hover around 2.3 million thanks to 14 losing seasons 1998–2011. The wild card berth in 2012 helped, but it will take on-field success to return attendance levels to those of the early 1990s.
Photo by: Roger Miller

Above and Right: Aerial views of Memorial Stadium, the home of the Orioles until replaced by the new Oriole Park at Camden Yards in 1992. Fans who had loudly voiced their dissatisfaction over the change were soon silenced by the easy access the downtown location provided and the sheer pleasure of watching a game at the new ballpark.
Photos by: Roger Miller

Left: The "Memorial Wall" at Memorial Stadium was a very large and visible concrete plaque located on the outside of the ballpark behind home plate. Its inscription read: "Dedicated as a memorial to all who so valiantly fought in the world wars with eternal gratitude to those who made the supreme sacrifice to preserve equality and freedom throughout the world—time will not dim the glory of their deeds." Before the stadium was demolished in February 2001, the wall was dismantled and preserved. Parts of it have been incorporated into a new Veteran's Memorial at Oriole Park at Camden Yards.
Photo: by Roger Miller

**MEMORIAL STADIUM
(1954–91)**
*Home of the Baltimore
Orioles*

Memorial Stadium, like the
city it served, was a no frills
place to watch baseball.
Originally built for minor
league baseball and professional football, an uncovered
second deck was added in
1954, when the Browns
moved to Baltimore from
St. Louis and became the
Orioles. Vice President
Richard Nixon threw out the
ceremonial first pitch on the
park's opening day. The park
was best known for its
meticulous field and devoted
fans, many of whom sneered
at plans in the early 1990s to
replace the worn stadium
with a downtown park.

Memorial Stadium was
home to Brooks Robinson
and Frank Robinson, where
Jim Palmer, Dave McNally,
Pat Dobson, and Mike
Cuellar each won 20 games
in the same year (1971),
where Cal Ripken's iron
man streak began, and
where Earl Weaver's
umpire-arguing, three-run-
home-run style of baseball
produced champions.

23

BOSTON RED SOX

FENWAY PARK

BOSTON RED SOX

Address:
4 Yawkey Way
Boston, MA 02215
Capacity: 37,493 (night), 37,065 (day)
Opening day: April 20, 1912—Boston Red Sox 7,
New York Highlanders 6 (11 innings)
Cost to construct: $650,000
Architect: Osborne Engineering Company
Dimensions (ft):
Left Field—310
Left Center—390
Center Field—420
Right Center—380
Right Field—302
Defining feature: Green Monster
Little-known ground rule: A ball going through
the Green Monster scoreboard, either on the bound or
fly, is two bases
World Series: 1912, 1914, 1918, 1946, 1967, 1975,
1986, 2004, 2007
All-Star Game: 1946, 1961, 1999

Memorable moments:
1914 July 11—Babe Ruth earns a victory as a pitcher in
his major league debut.
1918 September 11—Red Sox win the World Series
over the Chicago Cubs.
1960 September 28—Ted Williams hits a home run in
his final at-bat.
1975 October 21—Carton Fisk hits a 12th-inning home
run off the left field foul pole to win game six of
the World Series against the Cincinnati Reds.
1986 April 29—Roger Clemens strikes out 20
Mariners.
2004 October 23—The Sox win the first game of the
World Series and go on to lift the "Curse of the
Bambino" by beating the Cardinals 4-0.
2007 October 25—The Sox head for Denver leading
the Rockies 2-0 in the World Series. They win
4-0.

The Great Wall of China. The Wailing Wall in Jerusalem. The Green Monster in Fenway Park. Few structures in architecture, and none in baseball, are more identifiable than the 37-foot wall that separates Lansdowne Street from the outfield where Duffy Lewis, Ted Williams, and Carl Yazstremski once roamed.

A billboard for the greatness of baseball, the original wall, just 25 feet high, was probably built to keep residents in neighboring apartments from sneaking a free peak at the game. The Green Monster was expanded to its current height in 1934 and painted green in 1947. The seats built on top in 2003 have become among the most prized in baseball.

Fenway, the oldest of today's major league parks, is a living monument to baseball history. Babe Ruth's early pitching days, the Red Sox' dramatic—and final—World Series triumph in 1918, Jimmy Foxx and Ted Williams' slugging, Tony Conigliaro's beaning, Carl Yazstremski's left field mastery, Jim Rice's power, and Pedro Martinez's dominance, make it more than a "little lyrical bandbox of a ballpark," as John Updike famously described it.

Constructed in time for the 1912 season, the new ballpark was named by then Red Sox owner John I. Taylor because it was built in a marshy area of Boston known as the Fens. The opening was pushed off the front pages of Boston newspapers because of the *Titanic*, which had sunk just six days earlier. Mayor John F. Fitzgerald threw out the first pitch at the ceremony marking the park's opening, 48 years before his yet-to-be born grandson, John Fitzgerald Kennedy would win the presidency.

Before the Green Monster there was a steep mound of dirt that rose 10 feet to the left field wall, a fielding nightmare played so masterfully by Red Sox left fielder Duffy Lewis it was nicknamed "Duffy's Cliff." Fire has repeatedly reshaped baseball's most distinctive park. In 1926, the wooden bleachers along the left field line burned down, creating an opening that provided fielders a chance to catch foul balls outside the grandstand. Another fire in 1934 convinced the owners to replace wooden stands with concrete. It was post-World War II fire regulations that made the park's capacity, which once approached 48,000, shrink to the lowest of any park in the majors.

In a time-honored tradition, the park was also shaped to fit its talent. The bullpens were moved to right field in the 1940s to shorten the fences and take advantage of Williams' left-handed power. A bright red seat in the right field bleachers (Section 42, Row 37, Seat 21) marks the spot of Williams' longest Fenway blast, a 502-foot shot on June 9, 1946, off Fred Hutchinson of the Detroit Tigers. While balls fly over the Green Monster in left with regularity (a 23-foot tall screen was installed above the left field wall to protect windows across Lansdowne Street in 1936), no player has ever hit a home run over the right-field roof.

Today, the base of the left field wall is anchored by a manual scoreboard, which not only updates American League scores with 16-inch-high numbers (National League scores are electronic) but features two vertical strips which spell out the initials of former team owners Tom

Yawkey and Jean Yawkey—TAY and JRY—in Morse code.

Fenway has been around for most of baseball's history. However it did not witness a Red Sox world championship for many years after its infancy. On the afternoon of September 11, 1918, Les Mann, the Chicago Cubs leftfielder, tapped a ground ball to Sox second baseman Dave Shean, who tossed over to Stuffy McInnis for the out and a 2 to 1 victory. It would take more than eight decades and over 7,000 games before Fenway celebrated another World Series triumph. At a time when most classic ballparks have been shut down or destroyed, the Red Sox have resisted temptation to move to a new facility, and this was rewarded in 2004 when they defeated the St. Louis Cardinals to win their first World Series since 1918. Just to prove it was no fluke, they did the same thing in 2007, this time beating the Rockies 4–0.

Right: Postwar aerial view of Fenway Park before the extensive modifications to the stands. Note no bleachers on top of the Green Monster; these were added before the 2003 season.
National Baseball Hall of Fame

Left: A view outside Fenway Park as fans arrive for the game between the Red Sox and the Yankees on July 25, 2003. The Yankees won 4–3.
Photo by: Jerry Driendl/Getty Images

Right: Panoramic interior view of Fenway Park from the seats above first base during the July 25, 2003 Red Sox-Yankees game. Note the bleachers atop the Green Monster. Since the arrival of the new millennium there were ten years of renovations and improvements including three new HD video display and scoring systems, improved waterproofing, seat replacements, and a number of new features such as the new Home Plate Deck.
Photo by: Jerry Driendl/Getty Images

Right: Mounted police on crowd control outside Fenway Park in 1912.
National Baseball Hall of Fame

Far Right: A complementary pair to the last photograph. This one, some 40 years later, is a postwar view of Fenway Park that shows clearly some of the building that had taken place since 1912.
National Baseball Hall of Fame

Left: Fenway Park during the All-Star Game on June 20, 1999.
Getty Images

Right: Looking over the diamond toward the Green Monster, the lights illuminating play. It was just after the start of 1947 that workers started to install light towers at Fenway Park, allowing night games for the first time. The other major change for the 1947 season was the cleaning up of the left-field wall. All the advertisements were removed and the wall was painted green, thus creating the "Green Monster," such a defining feature of the ballpark. The photograph also highlights one of the problems with older ballparks: obstructed views by the 26 poles that hold the upper-deck up. From a very few seats, neither batter's nor pitcher's mound can be seen.
Digitalballparks.com

NEW YORK YANKEES

NEW YANKEE STADIUM

NEW YORK YANKEES

Address:
East 161st Street and River Ave.
Bronx, NY 10452
Capacity: 52,325 (50,291 seats)
Opening day: April 16, 2009—Cleveland 10, New York Yankees 2 1
Cost to construct: $1.5 billion
Architect: Populous
Dimensions (ft): these are as the old Yankee stadium
Left Field—318
Left Center—399
Center Field—408
Right Center—385
Right Field—314
Defining feature: Reinstating the distinctive copper frieze that lined the old stadium
Little-known ground rule: A ball hitting the foul pole in the 1930s was in play, not a homer
World Series: in the old stadium—1923, 1926–28, 1932, 1936–39, 1941–43, 1947, 1949–53, 1955–58, 1960–64, 1976–78, 1981, 1996, 1998–2001, 2003; in the new stadium—2009
All-Star Game: in the old stadium—1939, 1960, 1977, 2008

Memorable moments:
2009 April 3—First game in the new stadium is an exhibition game against the Cubs.
2009 April 16—MLB season opening day. A sellout crowd sees the Indians win.
2009 October 7—The new stadium's first playoff game sees the Yankees defeat the Twins thanks to two-run homers by Derek Jeter and Hideki Matsui.
2009 October 25—The Yankees win their first ALCS pennant since 2003 by beating the Angels 4–2
2009 November 4—The Yankees make their 40th World Series appearance a successful one by defeating the Phillies 7–3 on the night and 4–2. Andy Pettitte makes it a career total of eighteen playoff wins.
2013 April 12—The Yankees make their second ever triple play in a home game against Baltimore.

Few structures house more American memories than the old Yankee Stadium that was demolished at the end of the 2008 stadium. Ruth, Gehrig, DiMaggio, and Mantle are among the legends that have made history on these 10 acres in the South Bronx. Opened during the Harding presidency and still filling seats 13 presidents later, the majestic, triple-decked structure hosted heavyweight championships, fabled football games, international soccer matches, world leaders, two popes, Bruce Springsteen, and Pink Floyd.

Yankee Stadium became synonymous with the most successful sports franchise in America, hosting the World Series, on average, nearly every other year since it opened—so it was no real surprise when the new stadium opened to another World Series victory.

America was dotted with ballparks in 1923, when the Yankees opened the first baseball field to be dubbed a "stadium." Like the team that called it home, there was nothing modest or understated about its confines. Three decks of grandstands, originally intended to encircle the park to deprive non-paying bystanders a free look, rose above home plate, with a distinctive copper frieze decorating the roof of the top deck.

Babe Ruth himself, a left-handed hitter who is responsible for the short right field porch, hit the park's first home run to the roaring approval of the New York faithful, who quickly called it "the house that Ruth built."

It was here, just across the Harlem River from the Polo Grounds (which the Giants and even the Yankees once called home), that Joe McCarthy and Casey Stengel managed the Yankees to a combined 18 pennants, where Ruth hit his 60th and where Roger Maris hit No. 61. It was the home to Murderer's row, the Iron Horse, the Yankee Clipper, and the "Straw that stirs the drink."

Cemetery-sized monuments to Manager Miller Huggins and later Gehrig and Ruth were placed in deep center field, 10 feet from the wall. Patrons could pay homage to their heroes as they exited through the center field gate, and watch as balls hit sharply to center field occasionally rattled around gravestone-looking monuments. Plaques to DiMaggio and Mantle were added in 1969.

The legends were not limited to baseball. It was here on a cold November day in 1928, that Notre Dame coach Knute Rockne, facing an undefeated Army team, asked his players to "win one for the Gipper," which they did on a pair of second half touchdowns. It was here that the Baltimore Colts defeated the New York Giants in sudden death during the 1958 NFL championship, regarded as "the greatest game ever played." Joe Louis claimed the heavyweight championship of the world here. Pele scored goals. Pope Paul VI delivered mass in 1965, and Pope John Paul II did the same 14 years later.

Decades of use necessitated major renovations, and for the 1974 and 1975 seasons the Yankees played at Shea Stadium as their stadium underwent reconstruction costing at least 25 times more than the original park. The new stadium met mixed reviews. The copper frieze was replaced by plastic, the monuments in center field were moved beyond the outfield walls. Some complained that a baseball relic had been turned into another cookie-cutter design. Nonetheless, the upgrade added at least three

Left: Taken on Yankee Stadium's opening day, this photograph shows Jacob Ruppert, Jr.—the "Colonel"—an important NYC brewer and philanthropist, next to Kenesaw Mountain Landis (right)—baseball's first commissioner who was elected to office in 1920.
National Baseball Hall of Fame

Below: The outside of Yankee Stadium on opening day, April 18, 1923. It hosted nearly 75,000 fans.
National Baseball Hall of Fame

decades to the stadium's life, which ended with the 2008 season.

The new Yankee Stadium was built right next door and was ready for play in April 2009. The ground-breaking ceremony on August 16, 2006, coincided with the anniversary of Babe Ruth's death. Much of the new stadium provides a sense of continuity and echoes the old: a triumphal entrance, the limestone and granite outer wall, the field's dimensions, the location of the bullpens, Monument Park moved to the new stadium's center field wall—and the reinstating of the distinctive copper frieze that lined the old stadium until 1973. The new stadium boasts more legroom than the old; 56 luxury suites rather than 19; a bigger scoreboard, the New York Yankees Museum (located along the right field concourse), more retail outlets, and generally better amenities—but higher prices and fans' reactions have been mixed.

Success in the first season—including 87 home runs in the first 23 games and a World Series victory over the Phillies—have given the stadium a fantastic start.

Right: View from inside the stands over right field toward the diamond. Note the decorative cast-iron work on the roof edge. It was made of copper but painted white in the 1960s. It was removed in the 1970s while extra seating was being added to the upper deck. This would be echoed on the New Yankee Stadium, with a similar frieze made of steel painted white. Photo taken in 1947 during the World Series between the Yankees and the Dodgers.
Associated Press/National Baseball Hall of Fame

Far right: A panoramic view taken during a game between the Texas Rangers and the Yankees on April 12, 2000. The Yankees defeated the Rangers 8–6.
Photo by Al Bello/Allsport via Getty Images

Left: Yankee Stadium during the Mets-Yankees game on June 27, 2003. The Yankees won 6-4.
Photo by: Jerry Driendl/Getty Images

Left and Far Left: Two aerial views of Yankee Stadium. The first (left) was taken on September 9, 1928 and shows the Yankees playing the Phillies. The second photograph (far left) shows a 1960s view. Note the proximity of the New York City Transit's subway system: the 161st Street station today handles over 8 million passengers a year—the record is 8.8 million in 2012.
National Baseball Hall of Fame

Following page, Left: Another view of Yankee Stadium during the game against the Texas Rangers on April 12, 2000.
Photo by Al Bello/Allsport via Getty Images

Following page, Right: An exterior view of Yankee Stadium and its proud declaration of the 26 World Championships won there. The structure in the shape of a baseball bat was erected in front of the stadium in 1976. For fans, it was a popular meeting point. Its real function was to serve as an exhaust chimney for the stadium's boilers. The design was modeled after a Louisville Slugger, just like that used by Yankee Sluggers to win those 26 World Championships.
National Baseball Hall of Fame

Left: Great view inside the
new Yankee Stadium. Note
the frieze around the top of
the upper deck that recap-
tures the original stadium's
grandeur.
Photo by: Alex Jagendorf

TAMPA BAY RAYS

TROPICANA FIELD

TAMPA BAY RAYS

Address:
One Tropicana Drive
St. Petersburg, FL 33705
Capacity: 40,473
Opening day: March 31, 1998—Detroit Tigers 11, Tampa Bay Devil Rays 6
Cost to construct: $138 million
Architect: HOK Sport; Lescher & Mahoney Sports
Dimensions (ft):
Left Field—315
Left Center—370
Center Field—404
Right Center—370
Right Field—322
Defining feature: Left Field "Beach"
Little-known ground rule: A batted ball that hits either of the lower two catwalks, lights, or suspended objects in fair territory is a home run
World Series: 2008
All-Star Game: none

Memorable moments:
1999 May 2—Jose Canseco hits a towering blast onto a catwalk. When the ball doesn't come down, he is awarded a double.
1999 August 7—Wade Boggs gets his 3,000th hit, a home run.
2000 September 17—Devil Rays game with the Oakland Athletics is postponed because of Hurricane Gordon, only the third domed game ever postponed by weather.
2008 October 11—The Rays win game 2 of the ALCS in the eleventh after 5 hours and 27 minutes of play.
2008 October 19—The Rays beat the Red Sox 3–1 to take the AL Championship in front of 40,743.
2008 October 23—The Rays defeat the Phillies 4–2 to win game 2 of the World Series but lose the next three.

If you build it, they will come.

That was the hope of stadium investors and Florida baseball fans when the Florida Suncoast Dome (as it was then known) was completed in 1986. The state-of-the-art stadium had everything a modern park needed except a team. Business leaders tried to lure the White Sox, the Twins, and the Expos, but failed. A local businessman even purchased the San Francisco Giants for $113 million, but the move was rejected by major league owners. ("No team should be able to move nilly-willy," said Texas Ranger managing partner George W. Bush at the time.)

Major League Baseball finally rewarded Florida's baseball-starved fans the expansion Devil Rays in 1996, after owners agreed to spend $85 million to convert what had become known as the Thunderdome, home of the NHL Lightnings, into a baseball haven.

Purists frown on domed stadiums. Nevertheless, Tropicana Field, as it was named when it reopened, was made exclusively for baseball. Inspired by Ebbets Field, a grand, eight-story high rotunda greets fans as they enter.

The asymmetrical outfield dimensions closely match those from the old Brooklyn Dodger home. Seats are just 50 feet behind home plate, among the closest in the majors. To mimic the look of an outdoor stadium, the field features all-dirt base paths on artificial turf, the first major-league park to do so since St. Louis' Busch Stadium two decades earlier. The natural look is enhanced by FieldTurf, a new and realistic-looking form of synthetic grass that combines artificial grass with sand and ground rubber.

Dubbed "the Ballpark of the 21st Century" by team owner Vince Naimoli the year it opened, the stadium is loaded with amenities. The main rotunda features 1.8 million color tiles and a sound system delivering play-by-play of memorable baseball moments. The Center Field Street includes a cigar bar and restaurant, a billiards hall, a brew house, and a climbing wall. A restaurant in the batter's line of vision in dead center field is aptly named the "Batter's Eye." An area known as "The Beach" in left field's second deck features palm trees, a spa, a restaurant, and ushers dressed in Hawaiian shirts. A Devil Rays' home victory is announced to the outside by lighting the roof of Tropicana Field orange.

Tropicana Field has the world's second-largest cable-supported domed roof (after the Georgia Dome in Atlanta). The Teflon-coated fiberglass slants at a distinct angle. With hurricanes in mind, the roof is built to withstand wind up to 115 miles per hour. A versatile park, the stadium has hosted 16 other sports, including sprint car and motorcycle racing, gymnastics, tennis, weight-lifting, karate, motorcycle racing, equestrian events, track, figure skating, and ping pong.

There was a further $25-million facelift prior to the 2006 season; $10 million was spent on improvements during the same season; and further improvements were made in the offseason before the 2007 season.

In 2007 the Devil Rays dropped the Devil from their title and became the Rays. The results were immediate! in 2008 they reached the World Series, losing 4–1 to the Phillies.

Right: Inside the dome of Tropicana Field, home of the Tampa Bay Devil Rays since 1998.
Digitalballparks.com

Far left: Palm trees flank the entrance to Tropicana Field.
Digitalballparks.com

Left: Tropicana left field from upper deck. It's not the best ballpark in MLB. As Joe Mock of baseball.com said: "The Trop is a bad facility in a bad location." The attendance figures bear this out: half way through the 2014 season the Rays were being watched by an average of under 18,000—only Cleveland was worse.
Digitalballparks.com

TORONTO BLUE JAYS

ROGERS CENTRE

TORONTO BLUE JAYS

Address:
One Blue Jays Way Suite 3200
Toronto, Ontario M5V 1J1
Capacity: 49,539 for baeseball (up to 67,000 for other events)
Opening day: June 5, 1989—Milwaukee Brewers 5, Toronto Blue Jays 3
Cost to construct: $500 million
Architect: Rod Robbie and Michael Allen
Dimensions (ft):
Left Field—328
Left Center—375
Center Field—400
Right Center—375
Right Field—328
Defining feature: Retractable dome
Little-known ground rule: The decision as to whether a game begins with the roof open or closed rests solely with the Toronto Blue Jays. If the game begins with the roof closed: It shall not be opened at any time during the game
World Series: 1992, 1993
All-Star Game: 1991

Memorable moments:
1989 August 4—Blue Jay Pitcher David Stieb loses a no-hitter against the Yankees with two outs in the ninth inning on a Roberto Kelly double.
1989 October 7—Oakland's Jose Canseco hits a 500-plus foot home run into the fifth deck during game four of the league championship series.
1992 September 4—Blue Jays hit 10 consecutive hits against the Minnesota Twins, tying an AL record.
1993 October 23—Joe Carter's ninth-inning, three-run homer to the left field seats wins the World Series over Philly 8–6 for Toronto's second consecutive world championship.
1998 July 5—Roger Clemens records his 3,000th career strikeout.

Baseball has always been afraid of the elements, suffering through cold springs and canceling games in the rain. And then came SkyDome.

With its retractable roof, the first for any sports arena in the world, engineers figured out how to make baseball playable from April though October, even in the frigid north. Balancing 22 million tons 31 stories in the sky, SkyDome takes 20 minutes to open or close its four rooftop panels, which cover 340,000 square feet.

When it is open, downtown's trademark CN Tower looms over right field, and the downdraft makes home runs difficult. When it is closed, the dome is among the tallest in the majors, and the park turns into a hitter's field.

The perfectly symmetrical SkyDome was state-of-the-art when it opened, just six years before quirky Camden Yards would touch off a revival of uniquely shaped ballparks. The pitchers' mound is constructed on a fiberglass dish which allows it to be raised or lowered by hydraulics, and eight miles of zippers connect the strips of artificial turf .

Home to the Canadian Football League's Toronto Argonauts, SkyDome is more than just baseball. The building contains a 348-room Renaissance Hotel, with 70 rooms overlooking the playing field (where guests have exposed themselves in compromising positions more than once), a Hard Rock Cafe, a 300-foot bar with all seats facing the field, a health club with squash courts, a mini-golf course, and an indoor running track.

As much an architectural attraction as a sports venue, SkyDome was the first major-league park to exceed four million patrons in a single season, a feat it accomplished three years in a row. The stadium's $17 million, 33-foot by 110-foot Jumbotron video scoreboard with its 67,200 light bulbs is North America's largest.

The name SkyDome (not *the* SkyDome) was the product of a contest, selected from among 12,879 entries. The winner, Kellie Watson, was asked by the *Toronto Globe and Mail* to explain the name.

"It was dome," she responded, "where you could see the sky."

The SkyDome is now called Rogers Centre, honoring Rogers Communications, which now owns both the stadium and the Blue Jays. Following the demise of the Montreal Expos in 2004 and their reemergence as the Washington Nationals, the Toronto Blue Jays became Canada's only major league baseball team.

The 1992 and 1993 Blue Jays took back-to-back World Series titles, knocking off the Braves and Phillies, respectively. Since those glory years success has eluded the team, and there have been no return trips to the playoffs.

Known for its cheap tickets, bland concrete expanses, and fantastic retracting roof, the SkyDome (because that's what fans will always call it) has all the drawbacks of a multi-sport stadium—and all the benefits of a downtown location.

Right: External view of Toronto's SkyDome and the looming height of the CN Tower taken during the 1989 season.
Photo by Rick Stewart/Allsport via Getty Images

Right and Below: Two details of SkyDome. Note the base of the CN tower visible in the photo below. With the roof open, the downdraft from the tower makes batting a much more difficult job than when it's closed. *Digitalballparks.com*

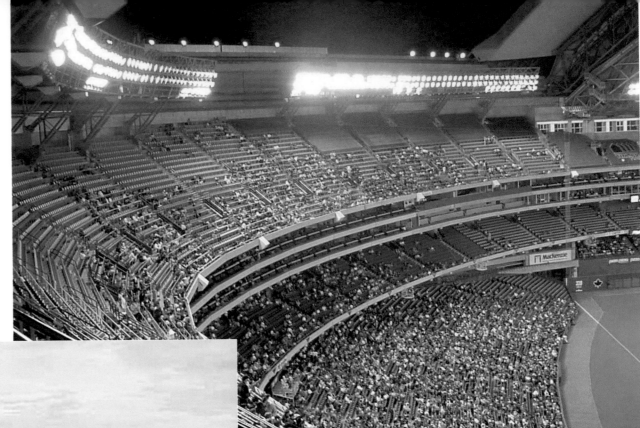

Above and Above Right:
Game 2 of the 1993 World Series between the Blue Jays and the Philadelphia Phillies on October 17. It ended a 6–4 win for the Phillies. Six days later Joe Carter won the sixth game, and the series, with a three-run home run. He had, the year before, caught the final out as first baseman.
Photo by Rick Stewart/Allsport via Getty Images

Left: Inside SkyDome with the roof open; photo taken in 1989 from above home plate. There have been a number of changes to the stadium since these photographs were taken, mainly since Rogers Communications bought the SkyDome for $25 million in January 2000. The main video board was upgraded from a JumboTron to a modern Daktronics board in 2005. A centre-field porch was added to the 200 level in 2013, the same year that Paul Beeston, President of the Blue Jays, said that the stadium needed $250 million in renovations. Surrounding the main scoreboard are the 70 rooms in the adjoining Rennaissance Hotel, that afford views of the playing area.
Photo by Rick Stewart/Allsport via Getty Images

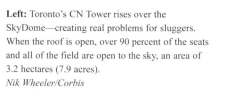

Left: Toronto's CN Tower rises over the SkyDome—creating real problems for sluggers. When the roof is open, over 90 percent of the seats and all of the field are open to the sky, an area of 3.2 hectares (7.9 acres).
Nik Wheeler/Corbis

They had the best of parks. They had the worst of parks. The ball fields used by the American League Central Division include Cleveland's Progressive Field, so lovely it sold out 455 consecutive games, and Minnesota's Hubert H. Humphrey Metrodome, a baseball design so hideous that even Twins fans demanded its demolition.

Today the American League Central Division includes one park from the 70s, two from the 90s, and two from the 00s. Though each offers its unique charms, Progressive Field, Detroit's Comerica Park, and Kansas City's Kauffman Stadium are all regarded as wonderful places to watch a baseball game. Chicago's U.S. Cellular Field—opened just a year before Baltimore's Camden Yards would incite a demand for old-fashioned retro-parks—is functional. And Minnesota's Hubert H. Humphrey Metrodome, with its dim lighting, its hefty bag outfield, and its bright, ball-losing, Teflon ceiling was barely that. The Twins finally managed to move in 2010—to the purpose-built Target Field. What a difference! The lack of a roof could sure be interesting in Minnesota's cooler periods. The rest of the parks of the Central Division should be around for a while.

U.S. Cellular Field from home plate upper level during the game between the Cleveland Indians and the White Sox on June 21, 2003. The White Sox won 4-3.
Photo by Jerry Driendl/Getty Images

CHICAGO WHITE SOX

U.S. CELLULAR FIELD

CHICAGO WHITE SOX

Aka: Comiskey Park 1991–2002
Address:
333 West 35th St.
Chicago, Ill 60616
Capacity: 40,615
Opening day: April 18, 1991—Detroit Tigers 16, Chicago White Sox 0
Cost to construct: $167 million
Architect: HOK Sport
Dimensions (ft):
Left Field—330
Left Center—377
Center Field—400
Right Center—372
Right Field—335
Defining feature: Exploding scoreboard
Little-known ground rule: Any fair, batted ball that travels over the yellow line painted on the outfield fence is a home run
World Series: 2005
All-Star Game: 2003

Memorable moments:
1993 April 9—Bo Jackson homers on his first major-league swing.
1993 June 22—Carlton Fisk catches his 2,226th game, a major-league record.
1997 June 16—The Cubs beat the White Sox 8–3 in Chicago's first regular season hometown matchup. The Sox come back to win the next two.
1998 July 31—Albert Belle establishes a major-league record by hitting his 16th home run of the month.
2002 September 19—Father and son spectators run onto field and attack Royals first base coach Tom Gamboa.
2005 October 2—The White Sox beat the Astros 6–7 to take a 2–0 lead in the World Series. They go on to win 4–0.
2008—The White Sox set a new season's home record at Cellular Field of 54–28.

The White Sox home was built under duress. Team owner Jerry Reinsdorf had issued the city an ultimatum: build a new ballpark or he'd take the team to Florida. The Illinois legislature resisted, but eventually agreed to build a park directly across the street from 80-year-old Comiskey Park, which Shoeless Joe Jackson and Luke Appling once called home and where Bill Veeck introduced the world to an exploding scoreboard and disco demolition night.

The new stadium saved baseball for Chicago's South Side. It also produced one of the most maligned ballparks of the modern era. Completed just one year before Camden Yards brought baseball back to the future, the park does not include many of the touches that have rendered new ballparks instant classics.

There is little inside to let you know that you are in one of America's great baseball cities. The field is almost exactly symmetrical. The top deck is far from the field, and rises at a harrowingly steep slope in order to expose the lower deck to the sky and make room for two tiers of money-making luxury boxes. How distant is the top deck? The front row of upper deck seats is further from the playing field than the back row at the Old Comiskey. Heavy winds off Lake Michigan have closed the upper deck on a few occasions for the safety of the fans.

Still, it was the first park built exclusively for baseball since Kansas City's Kauffman Stadium in 1973. Unlike its predecessor, there are wide concourses, lots of amenities, and no obstructed-view seats. The owners built a new exploding scoreboard, with pinwheels and fireworks set off by a White Sox home run. The retired uniforms of eight players are displayed at the park: Luke Appling (4), Nellie Fox (2), Minnie Minoso (9), Luis Aparicio (11), Ted Lyons (16), Billy Pierce (19), Carlton Fisk (72), and Harold Baines (3).

In its initial year, the reviews were not so bad, and 2,934,154 fans shattered the club's attendance record. It wasn't until Camden Yards opened the following year that fans began to realize what they had missed out on in Chicago.

The White Sox sold the naming rights to U.S. Cellular for 20 years at a price of $68 million in 2003, depriving baseball of one of its best known names (for all of his playing, managing, and owning days, what Charlie Comiskey is best remembered for is his stinginess toward his players that contributed to the "Black Sox" scandal of 1919.) The club has pledged to spend generously on stadium renovations. The fences have been moved in, a huge high-resolution video screen has been installed in the scoreboard, and a new fan deck, which allows fans to peer over the outfield from above the batter's line of vision in center field, has been added.

Just like old Comiskey, U.S. Cellular Field is a looming fixture on the Dan Ryan Expressway. For nearly two years, the two stadiums stood side-by-side, monuments to the past and the future, before wrecking balls did away with the past.

Whether the name change made the big difference or not, two years after becoming U.S. Cellular Field the White Sox recorded their first World Series win.

Left: For 80 years, until 1990, the home of the Chicago White Sox, Comiskey Park was also home to so many baseball greats, among them Shoeless Joe Jackson, Luke Appling, Nellie Fox, Minnie Minoso, and Luis Aparicio. The era of Bill Veeck's ownership, which began in 1959, saw such innovations as the "exploding" scoreboard, player names on the back of team jerseys, and special promotional events such as the disastrous Disco Demolition Night. *National Baseball Hall of Fame*

COMISKEY PARK
(1910–90)

Home of the Chicago White Sox.

Comiskey Park opened just a few years before today's surviving gems: Wrigley Field, Fenway Park, and Yankee Stadium. Comiskey was a much larger park, built to create long runs for outfielders and thrilling extra-base hits, rather than uncontested home runs. Pitchers loved it. The park was home to baseball's first All-Star game in 1933.

In 1960, Bill Veeck rigged the scoreboard to explode after every White Sox home run, a Comiskey tradition that continues today. Another promotion in 1979 didn't work out so well. Veeck invited fans to Disco Demolition Night, charging just 98 cents for bleacher fans who brought disco records to burn between doubleheader games. The outfield inferno resulted in 50 arrests, and White Sox were forced to forfeit the second game.

Above: Five-year-old Brian Jones sings the national anthem with his proud father, DeNard Jones, kneeling beside him.
Time Life Pictures/Getty Images

Right: A view from the press box at Comiskey Park during the 1959 World Series.
Time Life Pictures/Getty Images

Far Right: The new owner of the Chicago White Sox, Bill Veeck, standing in a snowy Comiskey Park.
Time Life Pictures/Getty Images

U.S. Cellular Field from press box level during the All-Star Game between the Indians and the White Sox on June 22, 2003.

Photo by Jerry Driendl/Getty Images

Right: Exterior of U.S. Cellular Field on June 22, 2003.
Photo by Jerry Driendl/Getty Images

Following page: This September 2013 view of U.S. Cellular Field was taken from the bleachers of Section 164 during a White Sox–Tigers game.
Mr.Konerko via wikicommons

Far Left: July 23, 1995—a view of Comiskey Park taken during a game between the White Sox and the Milwaukee Brewers. *Photo by Jonathan Daniel/Allsport via Getty Images*

Left: A satellite view of U.S. Cellular Field, I-94 and the Dan Ryan Expressway to the right. W35th Street runs along the top of the ballpark.

CLEVELAND INDIANS

PROGRESSIVE FIELD

CLEVELAND INDIANS

Aka: Jacobs Field 1994–2008
Address:
2401 Ontario Street
Cleveland, OH 44115
Capacity: 43,345
Opening day: April 4, 1994—Cleveland Indians 4,
Kansas City 3 (11 innings)
Cost to construct: $175 million
Architect: HOK Sports
Dimensions (ft):
Left Field—325
Left Center—370
Center Field—405
Right Center—375
Right Field—325
Defining feature: Left field scoreboard
Little-known ground rule: Thrown ball that
enters camera pits, dugouts, or diamond suites and
remains: two bases
World Series: 1995, 1997
All-Star Game: 1997

Memorable moments:
1994 April 4—Wayne Kirby's 11th-inning single gives
    Cleveland a 4-3 victory in the Jake's debut.
1995 September 8—Cleveland defeats Baltimore 3–2
    to clinch the AL Central Division, its first
    championship in 41 years.
1995 September 30—Albert belle hits 50th home run,
    most in Indians' history, until Jim Thome cracks 52
    seven years later.
1997 July 8—Hometown catcher Sandy Alomar hits a
    seventh-inning, two-run homer to lead the AL to a
    3–1 All-Star game victory.
2001 August 5—Trailing the Mariners 14–2, the Tribe
    scores 13 unanswered runs for their greatest
    comeback in 76 years.

They serve pirogues and sushi at the Jake. After playing for 61 years at cavernous Municipal Stadium at the edge of Lake Erie, derisively labeled the "mistake by the lake," the Indians moved into a boutique park where the blend of old and new is among the wonders of modern baseball.

Where the old stadium looked like something a child would build with an advanced erecter set, Jacobs Field was carefully sculpted to blend Indians' baseball with Cleveland's industrial roots.

The architects boast of using the city's traditional stone and brick masonry and providing direct views into the park from two street-level plazas to further integrate it with the city. Critics have credited the lattice work on the exterior for reflecting the bridges that cross the Cuyahoga River and the light standards for mimicking the industrial city's smokestacks. The result is an urban structure that is an integral part of Cleveland's downtown renaissance.

While the old stadium offered little more than a baseball diamond and seats, the Jake is a feast for the eyes. An appealing panorama of downtown Cleveland, if such a thing is possible, rises over the outfield, as does a 120-foot tall, 222-foot wide scoreboard, the largest freestanding scoreboard in the majors. The left-field scoreboard is reachable only by the likes of Mark McGwire, who did it off Orel Hershiser on April 30, 1997. Seats are angled to face the action at the plate.

Some elements resemble other parks. The 19-foot tall left-field fence, is referred to as the "mini-green monster." The bleachers compare to Wrigley's. Like most old parks, the playing field is anything but symmetric. Dead center field is not as deep as deepest left center. There is a triple deck in right. Home plate was transplanted from the old Municipal Stadium.

The new park is named after Richard Jacobs, who bought the Indians in 1985 and paid for the stadium's naming rights. The new home has suited the Indians well. Perennial losers, the Tribe won five consecutive division titles from 1995 to 1999. The stadium was sold out for a record 455 consecutive games, which would have been unimaginable at its old home.

Hitter-friendly Progressive Field was renamed after a local insurance company in 2008. It is one of the most attractive ballparks in Major League Baseball, offering spectacular views of downtown Cleveland. In 2008 readers of *Sports Illustrated* voted it the most beautiful. Architects HOK Sport, produced a design that included exposed steelwork to reflect the area's many bridges, and towers that echoed the city's smokestacks and skyscrapers.

Poor performances mean that attendance has been patchy of late. Half way through the 2014 season the Indians had attracted an average of just over 15,000 to their games giving a running total under a third of the top team, the Dodgers.

Right: Players line the baselines as a brass band prepares to play the national anthem before a game between the Kansas City Royals and the Cleveland Indians. The Indians won 11–2. *Photo by Tom Pidgeon/Getty Images*

Following page, Left: Bernie Williams—#51 of the New York Yankees—leaps up to catch a home run hit and misses the ball during the game against the Indians at Jacobs Field on May 26, 2001. The Yankees defeated the Indians 12–5. *Photo by Tom Pigeon /Allsport via Getty Images*

Following page, Right: General view of the stadium during the opening day game at Jacobs Field April 8, 2002. The Indians won 9–5. *Photo by Tom Pidgeon/Getty Images*

Right: Officially christened Lakefront Stadium when it opened in 1932, but more popularly known among fans of the resident Cleveland Indians as the "Mistake by the Lake," Municipal Stadium was used by the Indians until 1993.
National Baseball Hall of Fame

Far Right: After the last baseball game played in Cleveland Municipal Stadium in October of 1993, it continued in service as the home of the NFL Browns, until it was demolished in 1996 following the Browns departure for Baltimore. Now a new "Cleveland Browns" team plays in Cleveland Browns Stadium built in 1997 on the site of the original Municipal Stadium while the Cleveland Indians have played some of the best baseball in their long history at the critically acclaimed Jacobs Field since 1994.
National Baseball Hall of Fame

DETROIT TIGERS

COMERICA PARK

DETROIT TIGERS

Address:
2100 Woodward Ave.
Detroit, MI 48201
Capacity: 41,782 (seated) over 45,000 total
Opening day: April 11, 2000—Detroit Tigers 5,
Seattle Mariners 2
Cost to construct: $300 million
Architect: HOK Sports
Dimensions (ft):
Left Field—346
Left Center—402
Center Field—422
Right Center—379
Right Field—330
Defining feature: Scoreboard tigers
Little-known ground rule: Ball passing through
or under the bullpen fence: two bases
World Series: 2006, 2012
All-Star Game: 2005

Memorable moments:
2000 April 11—Fans endure 34-degree temperatures to
   watch the Tigers beat Seattle in the park's first
   game.
2000 August 23—Swarms of flying ants send fans
   fleeing.
2000 October 1—Shane Halter plays all nine positions
   on the final game of the season, the fourth major
   leaguer to do so.
2006 October 7—The Tigers beat the Yankees to take
   the divisional title 3–1.
2006 October 14—The Tigers sweep the Oakland As
   to reach the World Series but lose to the
   Cardinals.
2011 October 13—The Tigers win the fifth game of the
   ACLS to peg back the Rangers to 3–2, but go on
   to lose the next, and the series
2012 October 28—The Tigers lose another World
   Series as Giants win 4–3 in the tenth to go 4–0.

It is ironic that Detroit's baseball team moved from a place called Tiger Stadium. It is at Comerica Park that tigers roam.

Large tiger statues greet visitors outside. The perimeter is lined with tigers holding baseballs (actually lights) in their mouths. Two enormous tigers are positioned at either side of the scoreboard, who roar when the home team hits a home run. A merry-go-round featuring 30 hand-painted tigers entertains children along the first base side. There are even tiger claw marks scratched into concrete pillars around the park.

Comerica Park is a far cry from the no-nonsense, old-fashioned ambiance of Tiger Stadium which sat on the well-worn intersection of Michigan and Trumbull, a corner where baseball was played for more than a century. Comerica Park's Ferris wheel (carriages are shaped like baseballs), its multi-colored water fountain that shoots "liquid fireworks," the air-conditioned bar, enormous state-of-the-art scoreboard, and the lack of a single pillar to block the view, would have been unthinkable at Tiger Stadium.

Yet Comerica Park works to celebrate the city's rich baseball history.

Oversized sculptures cast in stainless steel along the center field wall show six Tiger greats in classic poses: Ty Cobb sliding spikes up, Willie Horton swinging, Al Kaline making a one-arm grab, along with Charlie Gehringer, Hank Greenberg and Hal Newhouser. Kaline's glove is positioned so that some day, some shot to deep center might just get caught.

The park's brick and steel construction and asymmetric dimensions mimic old parks, as does the dirt patch from the pitchers mound to home plate, a staple of turn-of-the-century fields. Originally the center-field flagpole was in play, just like at Tiger Stadium, though the fences were moved in and the flagpole now sits beyond the fence.

The park also frames a spectacular view of downtown Detroit, which has worked hard to keep baseball in the city.

The Tigers' earlier stadium—the famous Tiger Stadium—was one of the famous "Jewel Box" stadiums from before World War 1, built as Navin Field. Renamed Briggs Stadium in 1934 and Tiger Stadium in 1961, the ballpark witnessed six World Series appearances and titles in 1935, 1945, 1968, and 1984. Over 20 years later, Comerica Park saw the Tigers win their first AL pennant but lose to the Cardinals in the World Series—as they had done in 1934 and 1968.

The last few years have seen some changes to Comerica Park: the GM Fountain became the Chevrolet Fountain; 2012 saw renovation and upgrading of the left-field video display; and in 2014 a $4 million renovation to the Pepsi Porch was announced. On the field, the Tigers had a brilliant 2011 and 2012, winning back-to-back divisional titles, but losing out on the major prize, first being beaten 4–2 by the Rangers in the ACLS; then losing the World Series to the Giants 4–0.

Right: Comerica Park Entrance with Comerica Park Tigers by Michael Keropian.
Photo by: Richard Cummins/Corbis

TIGER STADIUM (1912–99)

Home of the Detroit Tigers

Tiger Stadium smelled like old-time baseball. The game was first played at the corner of Michigan and Trumbull, a healthy stroll from downtown, in 1896. Tiger Stadium, originally Navin Field, was opened in 1912, the same week the *Titanic* sank, and the same day that Fenway Park opened in Boston. By 1938, the stadium had been fully enclosed, able to capture the fragrance of hot dogs, peanuts, and Cracker Jack for thousands of games to come. The second deck provided some of the best seats in baseball, and produced dramatic home runs that would disappear into the upper stands. A 125-foot high, center field flagpole sat in fair territory along the center field fence until the 1930s.

Tiger Stadium remained a fixture through the careers of Ty Cobb, Charlie Gehringer, Hank Greenberg, Al Kaline, and Willie Horton. It was here, on May 2, 1939, that the Yankees Lou Gehrig asked to be removed from the lineup, ending his iron man streak at 2,130 games.

With its obstructed views and rusted pillars, Tiger Stadium was in need of major repair by the 1990s, when the Tigers considered enclosing it with a dome and finally decided that a new facility was needed. Today the stadium remains standing as city planners try to figure out what else belongs at the famed Detroit corner.

Right: c. 1937 aerial view of Tiger Stadium. The upper deck was constructed over the outfield bleachers in this year; and the 125-foot flagpole in center field was removed at the end of the season.
National Baseball Hall of Fame

The Final Game
Michigan & Trumbull
Sept. 27, 1999
Detroit vs. Kansas City

Left: Tiger Stadium taken on the occasion of the last game—Kansas City versus Detroit on September 27, 1999.
National Baseball Hall of Fame

KANSAS CITY ROYALS

KAUFFMAN STADIUM

KANSAS CITY ROYALS

Aka: Royals Stadium 1973–93
Address:
1 Royal Way
Kansas City, MO 64141
Capacity: 38,177
Opening day: April 10, 1973—Kansas City Royals 12, Texas Rangers 1
Cost to construct: $70 million
Architect: HNTB and Charles Deaton Design Associates
Dimensions (ft):
Left Field—330
Left Center—375
Center Field—400
Right Center—375
Right Field—330
Defining feature: Outfield waterworks
World Series: 1980, 1985
All-Star Game: 2012

Memorable moments:
1973 May 15—Nolan Ryan of the California Angels strikes out 12 Royals in his first of seven career no-hitters.
1976 October 3—George Brett hits an inside-the-park home run on a misplayed ball to edge teammate Hal McRae for the AL batting title in the season's final at-bat.
1977 May 14—Jim Colborn pitches Royal's first no-hitter at the stadium, beating Texas 6–0.
1980 August 17—George Brett's goes four-for-four and raises his batting average to .400
1985 October 27—Royals win their first World Series on Bret Saberhagen's game seven shutout over St. Louis.
1986 September 14—Bo Jackson hits his first major-league home run, a 475-foot blast believed to be the longest in stadium history.
1991 August 26—Bret Saberhagen no-hits the White Sox.
2013 September 22—The Royals win their 82nd game of the season, to ensure only their second winning season since 1994.

If baseball stadiums are urban cathedrals, then Kauffman stadium is a rogue church.

There is no Waveland Avenue or Lansdowne Street hugging the fence at Kauffman Stadium, just freeway and farmland. Approaching from the West, one could drive hundreds of miles without seeing lights as bright as the standards atop the stadium, which draw insects from acres around.

Yet it is orthodox baseball they worship inside, as devout as anywhere else. At a time when other cities were building multi-sports complexes, the Royals was the only franchise to build a baseball-only stadium during the 60s, 70s, and 80s. The site lines and seats all point toward the action. Grass replaced artificial turf in 1995, the fences were moved in, and the walls lowered.

Known for most of its life as Royals Stadium, it was renamed in honor of Ewing M. Kauffman who purchased the expansion team for Kansas City in 1968. If you want to date a color photo of Kauffman Stadium look at the seats. By the end of 2000, all of the red seats had been replaced by new blue ones. Intentionally located at the junction of I-70 and I-435, passersby can catch glimpses inside the park as they drive by.

If there is any monument to the era in which it was built, it is the 12-story high scoreboard, containing 16,320 lights, with a huge Royals crown on top, a Midwest version of Anaheim's Big A. The park's signature feature is a 322-foot wide water fountain spectacular—the largest privately funded waterworks in the world—which occupies the space that bleachers normally would, offering water-filled entertainment between innings.

Major work was carried out during 2007–2009 largely to improve and expand the fans' amenities and facilities. This work led to, among other improvements, wider concourses, new and better concessions, new press facilities, a state-of-the-art high definition scoreboard, and improved facilities for children. 2010 saw the Royals celebrate their thirty-eighth season at the stadium. Over sixty-three million fans have watched games here, and most would agree that it was a good place to watch baseball.

The improvements to the stadium ensured that the Royals extended their lease—due to run out in 2015—to 2030.

Above: A B-2 Spirit flies over the All-Star Game on June 10, 2012, as members of Team Whiteman (the Spirit is based at Whiteman AFB) hold the American Flag on the field. The 83rd annual MLB All-Star Game hosted 107 members of Team Whiteman who participated in the flag detail.
Photo by U.S. Air Force Airman 1st Class Bryan Crane

Right: All for a good cause! Some of baseball's premier power hitters stepped to the plate to support State Farm and MLB's effort to go to bat for charity. They raised $615,000 during the 2012 State Farm Home Run Derby.
Photo State Farm via wikicommons

Above: Night game at Royals Stadium.
National Baseball Hall of Fame

Far Left: General view of action during a game between the Red Sox and the Royals at Royals Stadium.
Getty Images

Left: The Truman Sports Complex comprises the Royals Stadium (lower) and Arrowhead Stadium, home of the NFL Kansas City Chiefs.
National Baseball Hall of Fame

MINNESOTA TWINS

TARGET FIELD

MINNESOTA TWINS:
HUBERT H. HUMPHREY METRODOME

Address:
3rd Avenue N
Minneapolis, MN 55415
Capacity: 39,504
Opening day: April 12, 2010—Boston Red Sox 2, Minnesota Twins 5
Cost to construct: $390 million
Architect: Populous
Dimensions (ft):
Left Field—339
Left Center—377
Center Field—404
Right Center—367
Right Field—328
Defining feature: Gates named after retired numbers—center field gate #3 (Harmon Killebrew); left field gate #6 (Tony Oliva); home plate gate #14 (Kent Hrbek); right field gate #29 (Rod Carew); plaza gate #34 (Kirby Puckett)
World Series: None
All-Star Game: 2014

Memorable moments:
2010 March 27—First game at the ballpark, a college baseball game between the University of Minnesota and Louisiana Tech.
2010 April 12—Jason Kubel hits the first home run at Target Field off Red Sox pitcher Scott Atchison.
2010 May 8—First doubleheader at Target Field, against the Orioles.
2010 October 6—The Twins play the first postseason game at Target Field, having won the Central Division championship. They lose to the Yankees.

Few stadiums in baseball were more maligned than downtown Minneapolis' dome. The Metrodome was loud, indoors, poorly carpeted, a hard place to spot balls, and a far, far cry from a field of dreams.

It was here that the underrated Twins won the World Series in 1987 and 1991 without winning a single game in a National League park. It was here that Kirby Puckett and Torii Hunter turned a flexible baggy-like wall into a tool of defensive beauty. It was here that the descendents of Harmon Killebrew and Tony Oliva played baseball for six (and sometimes seven) months a year in a climate better suited for hockey.

Few fields were more loaded with home-field advantages. The white Teflon roof made it difficult to pick up high-fly balls, particularly during day games. The screams of the homer hanky-waving fans in the 1987 World Series were measured by *Sporting News* at 118 decibels, about the same as a jet airplane on take-off. The odd curvature behind home plates made wild pitches routinely rebound toward first base.

The Twins used it to their advantage. In their first World Championship season in 1987, the Twins were 56–25 in the Metrodome during the regular season, and 29–52 on the road. They went on to win the World Series by winning every game at home, a feat they would repeat four years later, prompting many opposing fans to call for the dome's destruction. And the park was regarded as among the worst venues in baseball.

The Hubert H. Humphrey Metrodome, named after the former mayor, senator, and vice president, still stands, its Teflon-coated fiberglass ceiling rising almost 20 stories in the air. The roof came into play on numerous occasions. In 1992, Chili Davis hit a towering drive which bounced off a speaker dangling from the roof, which rather than being a home run, ricocheted into the glove of Baltimore second baseman Mark McLemore for an out.

Talk of a new stadium brewed in the Twin Cities for years. In the midst of playing some of their best baseball, but dogged by weak attendance and financial problems, the Twins were targeted in 2001–2002 by MLB for elimination (along with the Montreal Expos). The players union fought to stop the action, and the Twins were saved for the time being. The team continued its winning ways during and after the crisis, and its ownership stepped up efforts to get a new stadium. In 2005, the Twins and Hennepin County came to an agreement for building a 42,000-seat, open-air, downtown ballpark.

The ballpark was designed by Populous (called HOK Sport until 2009), the architects of Oriole Park at Camden Yards and PNC Park among others. Built at a cost of over $400 million, named after the Target Corporation in a deal announced on September 15, 2008, Target Field has no roof (both partners baulked at the extra $115 million cost) and so the Twins can enjoy the Minnesota elements, playing outdoors on grass for the first time in 28 years.

The stadium is equipped with a full roof-canopy soffit projecting out over the seating as well as "warming shelters" should the elements prove too much for the audience. Other facilities include the fourth largest scoreboard in MLB.

An overview of Target Field before the game on April 3, 2010. *Photo by: Lena Scherfenberg*

Above: 2010 panorama of Target Field.
Photo by: Robaato via wiki-commons

Right: Target Field Armed Services Appreciation Day, July 3, 2011. Opposite the photographer is the famous "Shaking Hands" logo that lights up when there's a Twins home run. Designed in 1961 by Ray Barton—who received the princely sum of $15 for the work—the logo has appeared on most of the Twins' uniforms ever since.
Photo by: JL1Row via wiki-commons

Far Right: Exterior view of the Metrodome.
Photo by: Joseph Sohm; ChromoSohm Inc./Corbis

The Hubert H. Humphrey
Metrodome in Minneapolis.
Getty Images

METROPOLITAN STADIUM (1961–81)

Home of the Minnesota Twins

The Met was the ultimate suburban stadium, built on developing farmland, where parking was plentiful and far from bustling downtown. Its hodgepodge of grandstands and bleachers, surrounding a perfectly symmetrical field, was the result of a quick transformation from a minor league to a major league park, speeded up to lure the Twins from Washington. The grounds crew had a reputation for tailoring the infield to suit their team, which hosted a World Series in 1965, the team's fifth year in the Twin Cities. Minnesota's northern climate made outdoor games a challenge in April and September, let alone October, and by the early 1980s the Twins were playing downtown under a dome. The Mall of America now thrives on the site where the Met once stood.

GRIFFITH STADIUM
(1911–61)
Home of the Washington Senators

"First in war, first in peace, and last in the American League," was the standing joke about the Washington Senators who spent half a century toiling in a ballpark so large that in four separate seasons the team could muster just a single home run in their home park.

It was at Griffith Stadium, about two-and-a-half miles from the White House, where William Taft became the first president to throw out a ceremonial first pitch, a ritual that was repeated by presidents through John Fitzgerald Kennedy. The centerfield indent, which made room for five duplexes that could not be razed, along with a large tree beyond the fence, gave the park a distinct character. The left field foul line, which at one point was 405 feet from home plate, made it a friendly park for pitchers, like Hall of Famer Walter Johnson, who called it home. Though the Senators had only fleeting moments of glory, it was also home to the successful Homestead Grays of the Negro League, and to Josh Gibson, who may have been professional baseball's finest power hitter.

After the 1960 season, the team moved to Minnesota and became the Twins. A new Senators team began playing at Griffith Stadium the very next year, but a desire for a more modern home prompted a move to Capitol Hill's RFK stadium. Griffith Stadium was knocked down in 1965.

Left: Just two-and-a-half miles from the White House, Griffith Stadium was the home of the Washington Senators for fifty years.For the 1961 season, the team moved to Minnesota and became the Twins. A new Senators team played at Griffith for a short time before moving to the newly built RFK Stadium. One of the distinctive features of Griffith was a 30-foot high wall that extended most of the length of right field, similar to famous "Green Monster" at Boston's Fenway Park. Griffith was knocked down in 1965.
Martin Luther King, Jr. Library/National Baseball Hall of Fame

Right: American baseball player Stanley "Bucky" Harris (1896–1977), playing for the Washington Senators, lands on home plate after scoring a home run during the seventh game of the World Series at Griffith Stadium, Washington, D.C., October 10, 1924. Washington won the game and the series.
Getty Images

Inset Right: Clark Griffith stadium, opening day, April 1, 1957.
Time Life Pictures/Getty Images

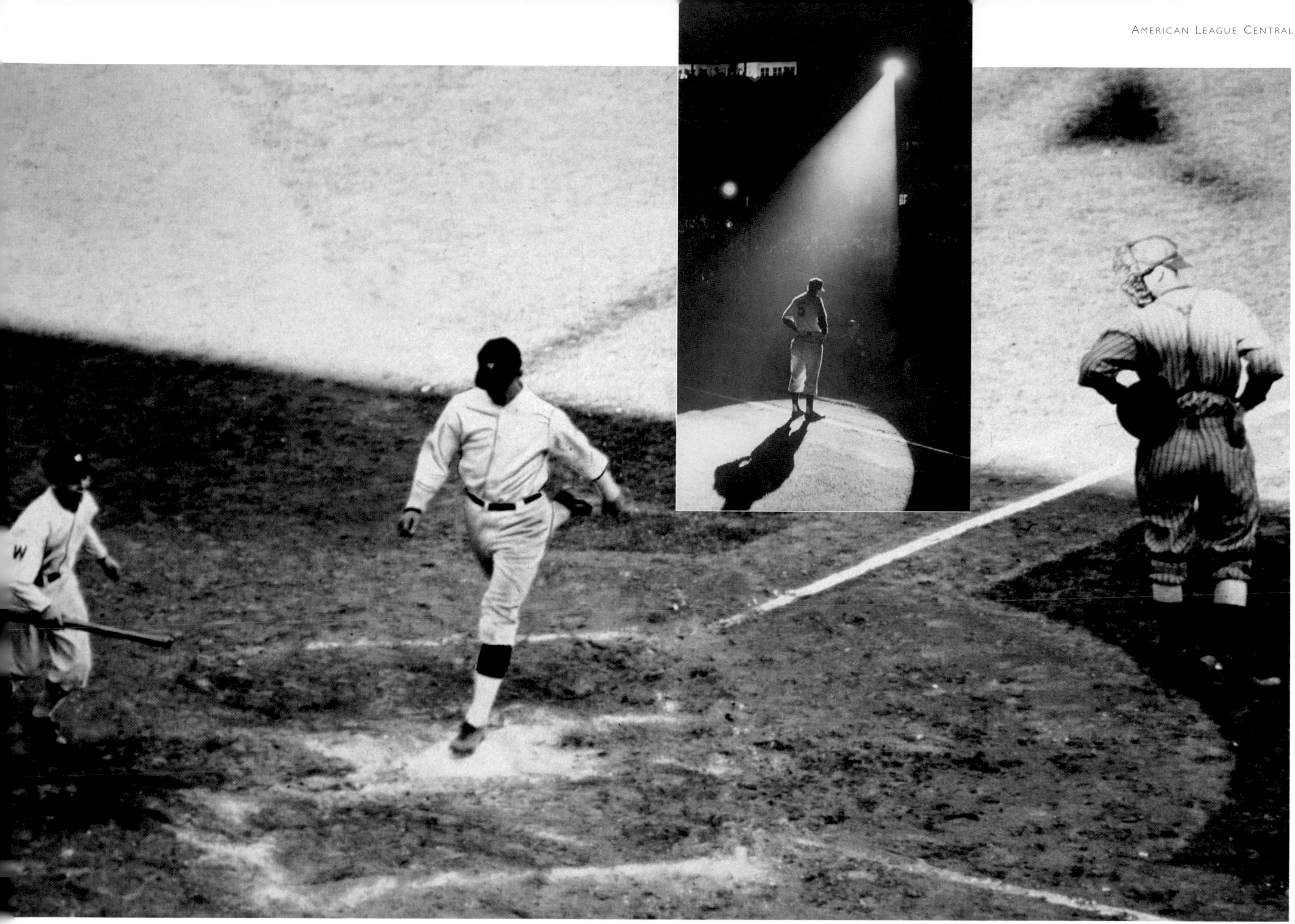

AMERICAN LEAGUE WEST

The teams of the American League West are relatively young and so are their stadiums. The Athletics, who originally played in Philadelphia in the early 1900s, before moving to Kansas City in the 50s, and eventually to Oakland, are the only exception. The LA Angels of Anaheim (originally the Los Angeles Angels, then the California Angels) came to life in the 60s, as did the Texas Rangers (from Washington), and the Seattle Mariners were born in 1977. The latest addition to the league, the Houston Astros, arrived for the 2013 season, their retractable-roofed Minute Maid Park having opened in 2000.

The Texas Rangers and the Seattle Mariners moved into new stadiums in the 1990s to rave reviews from their fans, who in the team's original homes had been subjected to Arlington's blistering heat and Seattle's impersonal dome. Anaheim has been quite comfortable in its home down the road from Disneyland since 1966. And Oakland A's fans enjoyed their oversized coliseum until the NFL Raiders returned in 1998, turning a baseball friendly stadium into a football arena uncomfortably forced to hold 82 baseball games a year.

The A's would like to build a park of their own—Cisco Field in Fremont was one idea—and have applied to do so. They'd like to be somewhere else soon; until then, the O.co Coliseum will be their home.

Right: The exterior of the Ballpark in Arlington before a game between the Seattle Mariners and the Texas Rangers on July 6, 2003. The Rangers defeated the Mariners 5-1.
Photo by Ronald Martinez/Getty Images

HOUSTON ASTROS

MINUTE MAID PARK

HOUSTON ASTROS

Aka: Enron Field 2000-2002
Address:
501 Crawford Street
Houston, TX 77002
Capacity: 40,950
Opening day: April 7, 2000—Philadelphia Phillies 4,
Houston Astros 1
Cost to construct: $248 million
Architect: HOK Sports
Dimensions (ft):
Left Field—315
Left Center—362
Center Field—435
Right Center—373
Right Field—326
Defining feature: Centerfield hill
World Series: 2005
All-Star Game: 2004

Memorable moments:
2001 July 18—Jeff Bagwell hits for the cycle as Houston
    beats St. Louis 17–11.
2001 October 4—Barry Bonds ties Mark McGwire's
    single season home run record, hitting No. 70 into
    the second deck.
2005 October 16—Astros take a 3–1 lead in the NLCS
    over the Cardinals. They go on to win 4–2.
2005 October 25—first World Series game to be played
    in Texas is also the longest World Series game ever
    played, lasting 14 innings and 5 hours and 41 min-
    utes. Astros lose 7–5.
2005 October 26—Astros lose a one-run game and the
    World Series to the White Sox 4–0.
2007 June 28—Craig Biggio hit his 3000th career hit, the
    first Astro to do so.
2008 November 16—Madonna performs a concert at
    the stadium as part of her Sticky & Sweet Tour.
2010 April 5—Opening Day sees highest attendance
    total ever, with 43,836 tickets sold.
2013 March 31—The Astros win their first game in the
    American League's West Division.

To appreciate the Astros' new home, think of the Houston Astrodome. Minute Maid Park is the opposite.

The Astrodome was a dark, completely enclosed, oversized gymnasium where power hitters went to die. Minute Maid Field is light, open, thoroughly unique, and conducive to scoring runs. Even when the retractable roof is closed, 50,000 square feet of glass panels allow patrons to gaze upon the Houston skyline or tropical storms passing above.

In its time, the Astrodome represented an amazing architectural achievement, allowing Houston fans to watch their team despite the swampy heat and mosquitoes of summer. Over time, it came to represent everything that modern baseball parks try to avoid.

Now, the Astros play in a state-of-the art structure where the roof alone cost about twice what it took to build the Astrodome. This is no cookie-cutter gymnasium. Its most unusual quirk, Tal's Hill —named after team president Tal Smith —is a grassy knoll in dead center field, that rises at a 20 degree angle to a height of about five feet, prompting the most graceful centerfielders to watch their feet as they chase down deep fly balls. On the left side of the incline is a flagpole, which is in play as at the old Tiger Stadium.

The left field bleachers are close, just 315 feet away, and protrude into the outfield, creating funny bounces and fantastic views. A one-of-a-kind porch hangs out over the outfield action, where walls come in several different shapes and heights. Small foul territories bring fans close to the field.

The park's signature feature is a 57-foot, 24-ton, 1860s steam locomotive, which chugs down an 800-foot track along the left field roof when the Astros do something special. Trains are a motif throughout the stadium. Most fans enter through the 1911 vintage Union Station, which forms the park's main entrance. The scoreboard is baseball's biggest, and explodes in celebration of every Astros' home run.

The park opened as Enron Field, after the Houston-based energy conglomerate which paid $100 million for 30 years of naming rights. At the park's opener, with soon-to-be President Bush on hand, Enron President Ken Lay threw out the ceremonial first pitch. Two years later, the energy conglomerate had gone bankrupt amid scandal. The large Enron sign remained on the park until the Astros bought back the naming right. Months later, they sold the rights to Minute Maid.

Minute Maid Park is a hitter-friendly ballpark, particularly in left field, which is just 315 feet away. Fielding is also made trickier in centerfield, thanks to Tal's Hill which is a piece of ground 90 feet wide withs an incline of 30 degrees—just to make the fielder's job a little more difficult.

From 2013 the Astros started a new life with a change of ownership and a change of league, moving to the American League West. Unforunately for the fans, this didn't improve the teams's fortunes as they endured their third season with over a hundred losses.

Right: Enron Field became Minute Maid Park for the 2003 season after an accounting scandal bankrupted the Houston-based energy conglomerate. This photograph shows off well Tal Hill at Minute Maid Park; note also the flagpole, which is in play.
National Baseball Hull of Fame

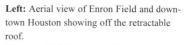

Left: Aerial view of Enron Field and downtown Houston showing off the retractable roof.
Photo by: Bob Daemmrich/Corbis

Opposite: Minute Maid Park-view toward first base from third base.
Digitalballparks.com

Left: This photograph of Minute Maid Park affords a view of the 57-foot, 24-ton full-size replica steam loco that runs on an 800-foot track above left field. The park has a strong railway connection: the main entrance is the 1911 Union Station.
Digitalballparks.com

Astrodome (1965–99)

The Houston Astrodome was hailed as the eighth wonder of the world when it opened, an architectural achievement that would change baseball's relationship to the elements. During the dome's 35-year baseball history, the Astros were rained out once, an enormous 1968 storm which didn't dampen the field, but prevented fans and the umpiring crew from making it to the park. Like a giant gymnasium, the Astrodome provoked awe in visitors who had never imagined indoor baseball, or an animated scoreboard with dancing figures for entertainment.

The Astrodome's field was originally grass, but the transparent roof created a menacing glare. The darkened panes killed the grass, and prompted the need for Astroturf, which become a standard for many other sports venues. Besides baseball, the Astrodome was host to musicians including the Rolling Stones, boxing matches, tennis tournaments, and the 1992 Republican National Convention.

Left: Aerial view of the Houston Astrodome, photographed in 2000. Photo by Paul S. *Howell/Getty Images*

Right: The Houston Astrodome was the home of the Astros for 35 years 1965–2000. *National Baseball Hall of Fame*

Left: A view of the Houston Astrodome during a game between the Chicago Cubs and the Houston Astros on August 29, 1996. The Cubs won the game 4–3.
Getty Images

Right: Houston Astrodome opening night of April 9, 1965, playing the Yankees in an exhibition game in front of President Lyndon B. Johnson.
National Baseball Hall of Fame

LOS ANGELES ANGELS OF ANAHEIM

ANGEL STADIUM OF ANAHEIM

LA ANGELS OF ANAHEIM

Aka: Edison Field (1998–2003), Anaheim Stadium (1966–1997)
Address:
2000 Gene Autry Way
Anaheim, CA 92806
Capacity: 45,389
Opening day: April 19, 1966—Chicago White Sox 3, California Angels 1
Cost to construct: $24 million
Architect: Robert A.M. Stern, HOK (renovations)
Dimensions (ft):
Left Field—330
Left Center—365
Center Field—400
Right Center—365
Right Field—330
Defining feature: The Big A
World Series: 2002
All-Star Game: 1967, 1989, 2010

Memorable moments:
1973 September 27—Nolan Ryan strikes out 16 Twins to establish a new record of 383 season strikeouts.
1984 September 17—Reggie Jackson hits his 500th home run, 17 years to the day after hitting his first, and in the same park.
1985 August 4—Rod Carew hits his 3,000th career hit.
1986 June 18—Don Sutton wins his 300th game against Texas.
1986 October 12—Dave Henderson hits a two-out, two-run homer off Donnie Moore, to defeat the Angels who were within one strike of their first World Series appearance.
1990 September 14—Ken Griffey Jr. and Ken Griffey Sr. become first father-son pair to hit back-to-back home runs.
2002 October 27—Garret Anderson's bases loaded double in the third inning breaks a 1–1 tie and leads the Angels to a 4–1 win over the San Francisco Giants in game seven of the World Series.

Like much of Orange County, Angel Stadium was built on an old citrus grove, where oranges, alfalfa, and corn once grew. Anaheim in the 1960s was rapidly shedding its rural past. When Anaheim Stadium, as it was then known, opened in 1966, Disneyland had been open for just a decade, and nearby Los Angeles was spreading without restraint.

In that context, the preposterously enormous, 230-foot "A" reaching over the left-field wall to the sky, with a huge scoreboard and Standard Oil advertisement in the middle, and a golden halo on the top, fit right in. Roughly modeled on Dodger Stadium, the state-of-the-art National League park where the Angels had spent the previous four seasons, the team's new home provided an identity for the "California Angels," owned by singing cowboy Gene Autrey.

The park had a distinct Southern California charm, palm trees, wide open concourses, and immaculate concession stands, a far cry from the urban grit of eastern parks. The location was selected for its suburban ease, its ready freeway access and abundant parking.

The inside was made for baseball and nothing else. Short walls left outfielders to battle spectators for long fly balls. The triple deck contained no obstructed views. For its first two decades, the stadium had no bleachers at all, leaving the "Big A," and sometimes the distant San Gabriel mountains, looming as California icons.

The panoramic views ended after the 1979 season when the stadium was enclosed to add 20,000 seats for the NFL's Los Angeles Rams. The "Big A" was moved to the parking lot, where it remains today. In the 1990s, the Rams departed for St. Louis, the Disney Corp. assumed control of the Angels, and renovations were once again underway. This time $100 million was spent returning the park to its baseball-only status.

The 20,000 football seats were replaced with bleachers, a state-of-the-art scoreboard, and the "California spectacular," an improbable backdrop of geysers shooting water 90 feet in the air, waterfalls flowing down a rocky mountainside, artificial rocks, real trees, and the look of something straight out of Disneyland. Three full-service restaurants were added.

After nearly four decades of baseball in Anaheim, the Angels finally reached the World Series in 2002, which they won in dramatic style against the Giants in game seven, at home.

In spite of its age—and the lack of a playoff game since 2010—the stadium continues to attract an average of over 40,000 fans to every game.

Below Left: The Big A sign gives Angel Stadium its nickname. The halo lights up when the A's win. *Photo by Buchanan-Hermit via wikicommons*

Below: Looking across the outfield to the unusual "California Spectacular" from where A's home runs and victories are feted by geysers and fireworks. The scoreboards were updated by Daktronics in 2004. At right, the main board has three electronic displays, the Prostar Display in the center is 42ft high by 67ft wide and alongside are two 11ft by 50ft displays. Opposite the camera is the Angel Vision Prostar video display, with two trivisions on each side. Atop the structure above the video board is an illuminated Angels "A." *Photo by Amin Eshaiker vis wikicommons*

Following pages, Left and Right: Anaheim Stadium became Edison International Field in 1996 under a $50 million, 20-year sponsorship deal. After five years, on December 30, 2003, the Angels announced that they were going to rename their ballpark Angel Stadium of Anaheim for the 2004 season because Edison had decided to opt out of its naming rights agreement. *Photos by Jed Jacobsohn/Allsport via Getty Images (both)*

OAKLAND A'S

OAKLAND-ALAMEDA COUNTY COLISEUM

OAKLAND A'S

Aka: Oakland-Alameda County Stadium (1968–97, 2008–11), Network Associates Coliseum (1998–2004), and McAfee Coliseum (2004–2008)

Address:
UMAX Stadium, 1998
7000 Coliseum Way
Oakland, Ca. 94621

Capacity: 34,000 (for baseball)

Opening day: April 17, 1968—Baltimore Orioles 4, Oakland Athletics 1

Cost to construct: $25.5 million

Architect: Skidmore, Owings & Merrill

Dimensions (ft):
Left Field—330
Left Center—362
Center Field—400
Right Center—362
Right Field—330

Defining feature: Mount Davis

World Series: 1972, 1973 1974, 1988, 1989, 1990

All-Star Game: 1987

Memorable moments:
1968 May 8—Catfish Hunter pitches a perfect game against the Minnesota Twins.
1972 September 22—Gene Tenace hits two RBI to lead Oakland to a 3–2, World Series game seven victory over Cincinnati.
1979 April 17—Just 653 fans show up to watch the A's beat the Mariners 6–5.
1988 October 18—Mark McGwire's ninth-inning home run defeats Dodgers in World Series game three.
1991 May 1—Rickey Henderson steals third base for his 939th stolen base, breaking Lou Brock's record.

It is not with affection that A's fans refer to the dreary slab of luxury boxes, clubs, and sky high grandstands which killed the bleachers, the ice plants, and the view of the East Bay hills, as "Mount Davis." While the rest of the country was making their ballparks better, Oakland was going in the opposite direction.

The Oakland-Alameda County Stadium, as it was known until 1998, had always been a workmanlike like place to see a baseball game. Huge foul territories annoyed batters and kept fans too far from the action. The symmetry reflected the era in which it was built. It looked less like a ballpark than a coliseum.

But except for the distances, there wasn't a bad seat in the house. The plain concrete confines were accessible, the bleachers relaxing, and the view of the Oakland hills, scarred by a huge quarry in dead center, let you know that you were in one of baseball's finest climates.

And then Al Davis brought the Raiders back to Oakland.

The bleachers are now gone. The stadium is enclosed. And the new scoreboards are in perfect position only for a game with two end zones. The seats atop Mount Davis offer sweeping vistas of Mt. Tamalpais 20 miles in the distance, but no view of the warning track just below. Adding insult to the aesthetic change, the renovations weren't finished in time for the A's to begin their 1996 season, forcing them to open at a minor league park in Las Vegas. When fans were finally allowed back in (30 years to the day after then-Governor Ronald Reagan had thrown out the ceremonial first pitch at the stadium's inaugural game) they were given yellow construction hats with an A's logo.

The lack of collegiality between the football and baseball clubs is apparent on the A's Internet page, which refers dismissively to the coliseum as home to the Oakland Athletics and "Oakland's NFL franchise."

On the playing field, the wide foul territory is said to cost a batter five to seven batting average points over the course of a season, though it did not stop Reggie Jackson, Rickey Henderson, Jose Canseco, Mark McGwire, or Jason Giambi from hitting their stride. To the joy of most hitters, the fences have been moved in from their original locations, and the football enclosure keeps the wind down.

This was the home of Charlie Finley's innovations: orange baseballs, which were used in a 1973 exhibition game against the Indians, and gold-colored bases which adorned the infield for opening day 1970, a move the no-nonsense officials at Major League Baseball quickly banned. Besides the A's and Raiders, the coliseum was home to the USFL Oakland Invaders and has hosted scores of concerts from the Rolling Stones and the Who, to the Grateful Dead, Bruce Springsteen, and Bob Dylan.

Local lore has it that the coliseum was home to baseball's first "wave," on October 15, 1981, set off by the blond-haired, dugout-hopping, drum-pounding, wild man known as "crazy George," a development reviled by some baseball fans almost as much as "Mount Davis."

For the last ten years A's fans have expected a new ballpark but still have no idea where their team will be playing in the future. The concrete O.co Stadium is showing its age and the A's would

like a dedicated stadium. But where do they move? The location the owners want (near San Jose in the lucrative heart of Silicon Valley) is within the territory of the Giants who are playing hardball. They don't want to give up the rights to that area to another MLB team who will start encroaching on their fan base. The proposal to move has spent five years gathering dust—so much so that San Jose has filed a lawsuit against MLB for the loss of earnings. But Oakland, too, wants to keep the team and a waterfront property is being promoted—this has MLB support but owner Lew Wolff has been inplacably opposed. This confused situation will need resolving soon.

Below: Fans sing "Take Me Out To The Ballgame" during the seventh-inning stretch at Oakland Coliseum 2000.
San Francisco Chronicle

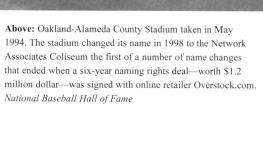

Above: Oakland-Alameda County Stadium taken in May 1994. The stadium changed its name in 1998 to the Network Associates Coliseum the first of a number of name changes that ended when a six-year naming rights deal—worth $1.2 million dollar—was signed with online retailer Overstock.com.
National Baseball Hall of Fame

Left: The Coliseum before the start of a game between the Oakland Athletics and the Montreal Expos on June 15, 2003. The Athletics defeated the Expos 9-1. *Photo by: Justin Sullivan/Getty Images*

Far Left: The Coliseum is dual-use with both football and baseball played. This shows the Coliseum during an NFL game between the Oakland Raiders and the Baltimore Ravens on December 14, 2003. *Getty Images*

SEATTLE MARINERS
SAFECO FIELD

SEATTLE MARINERS

Address:
First Ave. S and S. Atlantic St.
Seattle, WA 98104
Capacity: 47,116
Opening day: July 15, 1999—San Diego Padres 3, Seattle Mariners 2
Cost to construct: $517 million
Architect: NBBJ
Dimensions (ft):
Left Field—331
Left Center—390
Center Field—405
Right Center—387
Right Field—327
Defining feature: Open-sided retractable roof
Little-known ground rule: If the roof is open and climatic conditions warrant it, the roof can be closed in the middle of an inning. Once the roof is closed during a game, it will not be re-opened. If a game begins with the roof closed, it may be opened only between innings and the visiting team may challenge the decision to open it
World Series: None
All-Star Game: 2001

Memorable moments:
2000 August 1—Mike Cameron hits a 19th-inning home run to beat Boston 5–4.
2000 September 30—Alex Rodriguez hits two home runs and bats in seven runs to beat the Angels and move Seattle into a first place tie.
2000 October 6—Carlos Guillen scores Rickey Henderson on a ninth-inning squeeze bunt to sweep White Sox in the division playoffs.
2001 July 11—Cal Ripken, in his final All-Star game, hits a third-inning home run and is named the game's MVP.
2001 October 6—Mariners win their 116th game, tying the Chicago Cubs major-league record.

It took $517 million to move Seattle fans from baseball's worst stadium to one of its best, about the same dollar amount it took to construct every major-league park built in the United States through 1990—combined.

Real grass. Cedar-lined dugouts. Elevated bullpens. An old-fashioned, hand operated scoreboard and 11 video display boards. A concourse where fans waiting for salmon sandwiches, clam chowder, sushi rolls, or garlic fries won't miss the action.

There are 600,000 bricks in the facade, 40 miles of piping, 150 miles of electrical wiring, 200 miles of concrete, 535 metal halide lights, 600 tons of infield clay, and 20 to 30 miles of heating coils for the turf, which is a blend of Kentucky Bluegrass and perennial rye. And it wouldn't be Bill Gates' Seattle without Internet kiosks and luxury suites with high speed Internet access.

But what really cost money was the roof, which opens and closes like a well-vented convertible, covering the stands and the field, but leaving the side open to allow fresh air to blow in. When the roof is open, the right side of the upper deck offers views of downtown and the Puget Sound, though the city's landscape is not visible from most of the stadium.

The confines, though not the major leagues' coziest, are a vast improvement over the dark and cavernous Kingdome, the Mariners' previous home. The design offers a more mobile way to watch baseball. Wide concourses with lots of concessions and site lines allow people to move around during the game. The park also features one more women's bathroom than men's, which may be a first at a sports venue. Its restaurants, and even the field, are available for weddings, Bar Mitzvahs, and other events (for a substantial sum) when games are not being played.

The state-of-the-art park was built, owners said, to lure fans who in turn would bring in enough revenue to pay top-notch players to build a great team. Ironically, the stadium's astronomical cost put a serious dent in the owner's wallet, and now some of the Mariners' greatest, including Randy Johnson, Alex Rodriguez, and Ken Griffey Jr., have found homes elsewhere.

Right: Seattle is a fabulously beautiful city. Here the city's two main stadiums—the NFL Seahawks Stadium (closer to the camera) and Safeco Field, current home of the Seattle Mariners—are seen under white-topped mountains on June 25, 2003. The Seahawks stadium opened on July 19, 2002; Safeco on July 15, 1999.
Photo by Otto Greule Jr/Getty Images

Left: The Seattle Mariners play the Texas Rangers. *Photo by: Paul A. Souders/Corbis*

Left: Exterior view of Safeco Field on June 25, 2003.
Getty Images

This page: Safeco Field with roof retracted. Built to the south
of the Mariners' old home, the Kingdome (see next page), the
new stadium was named after Safeco, a financial services
company whose roots in Seattle date back to 1923. Safeco will
pay $1.8 million per year for the next 20 years.
Photo by Otto Greule Jr/Getty Images

Left: When it opened in 1977, the Kingdome was the American League's first indoor stadium. In 1994 four ceiling tiles fell before the start of a game causing the team to play its final 15 games on the road. Repairs cost $70 million. The stadium, then home to the NFL Seahawks as well as the Mariners, was spectacularly demolished in 2000. A new football only stadium now occupies the site.
National Baseball Hall of Fame

Right: The dome itself was 660 feet in diameter and 250 feet from its apex to the playing surface. A batted ball hitting one of the speaker assemblies hung from the dome was considered to be in play. More than one hitter was "robbed" of a home run when a ball bouncing off a speaker was caught in flight for an out. Note the proximity to Puget Sound.
National Baseball Hall of Fame

TEXAS RANGERS

THE BALLPARK AT ARLINGTON

TEXAS RANGERS

Aka: The Ballpark in Arlington (1994–2004), Ameriquest Field in Arlington (2004–06), Rangers Ballpark in Arlington (2007–13)

Address:
1000 Ballpark Way
Arlington, TX 76011
Capacity: 49,292
Opening day: April 11, 1994—Milwaukee Brewers 4, Texas Rangers 3
Cost to construct: $191 million
Architect: HKS, Inc. and David M. Schwarz Architectural Services
Dimensions (ft):
Left Field—332
Left Center—390
Center Field—400
Right Center—381
Right Field—325
Defining feature: Center field office building
Little-known ground rule: Ball lodging in outfield fence padding or in the manually operated scoreboard in left field fence is a ground rule double
World Series: 2010, 2011
All-Star Game: 1995

Memorable moments:
1994 June 13—Jose Canseco hits three home runs and drives in eight runs in a 17–9 victory over Seattle.
1994 July 28—Kenny Rogers throws a perfect game against the Angels, the first Ranger to do so.
1996 April 19—Juan Gonzelez, Dean Palmer, and Kevin Elster combine for 16 RBI as the Rangers beat O's 26–7.
1997 June 12—In baseball's first regular-season interleague game, San Francisco beats the Rangers 4–3.
2010 October 22—Victory over the Yankees in the sixth game of the ALCS wins the Rangers their first American League pennant.
2010 October 30—The Rangers win the first World Series game ever won by a team from Texas, beating the Giants 4–2.

Take a bit of Ebbets Field, some Tiger Stadium, a little Yankee Stadium, some Wrigley Field, and a touch of Camden Yards. Mix in a lot of Texas, put it in a suburban parking lot, and you approach the Ballpark at Arlington.

The asymmetrical outfield is like Ebbets Field, with eight facets sending hard-hit balls in different directions The double-decked, right-field porch is like Tiger Stadium, though it is too deep to catch as many home runs. The bleachers recall Wrigley. The canopy lining the upper deck is reminiscent of Yankee Stadium. The brick arches on the exterior feel like Camden Yards.

Yet this is Texas. Cast iron Lone Stars adorn aisles seats, replicating those on the building's facade. Large steer skulls and murals depicting the state's history decorate the walls, and a brick "Walk of Fame," celebrating Ranger's history surrounds the park. The grass in the batter's line of vision in dead center is named Greene's Hill after former Arlington Mayor Richard Greene. There is a Texas-sized dimension to the entire stadium complex, which includes a 12-acre, man-made lake (named for late Rangers broadcaster Mark Holtz), a 17,000 square-foot baseball museum said to be the largest outside Cooperstown, a 225-seat auditorium, a children's learning center, a four-story office building, and a kid-sized park with seats for 650 just outside.

To battle the Texas elements, the stadium is sunken, out of the wind, and enclosed by the office building, home to the Ranger's front office, just beyond center field. A giant wind-screen, 42 feet high and 430 feet long, was installed on the roof to further reduce wind. Overhead fans in the upper and lower deck porches help keep patrons cool.

The $191 million park was paid for largely through a sales tax increase, pushed through by the team's managing partner in the early 1990s, George W. Bush.

With six postseason appearances, including two World Series, between 1996 and 2012, the Rangers have an excellent playing record in recent years. Their hitter-friendly ballpark has certainly helped, with eight 200+ home run years 1996–13, including the remarkable 260 in 2005. The Texas temperatures still lead to the question of why there is no roof, but renovations in 2010–11, including new Daktronics displays ensure that the ballpark is up to date.

In February 2014 the Globe Life and Accident Insurance Company—based in Dallas—bought the naming rights to the stadium.

Right: Texas sized in every way, this is how the Ballpark at Arlington appeared when constructed. It boasted a 12-acre man-made lake, a baseball museum said to be the largest after the Hall of Fame in Cooperstown, and a four-story office building. Since February 2014 it has been named after Globe Life.
National Baseball Hall of Fame

1998 view of the Ballpark in Arlington.
Joseph Sohm; Visions of America/Corbis

Left: To provide the players some protection from the harsh Texas winds, the playing field is sunken and surrounded by tall, wind blocking structures and screens.
National Baseball Hall of Fame

Far Left: A general view of the exterior of the Ballpark in Arlington before a game between the Seattle Mariners and the Texas Rangers on July 6, 2003. The Rangers defeated the Mariners 5–1.
Photo by Ronald Martinez/Getty Images

Following page, Left: Another view of the Ballpark in Arlington on July 6, 2003.
Photo by Ronald Martinez/Getty Images

Following page, Right: Heavy clouds loom over the ballpark during play between the Seattle Mariners and the Texas Rangers at the Ballpark in Arlington on July 6, 2003.
Photo by Ronald Martinez/Getty Images

The National League of Professional Baseball Clubs, now known simply as the National League, was formed in 1876, the year of Custer's last stand, and exactly 100 years after the United States declared its independence. Some of its eight charter cities are familiar baseball towns: Chicago, Cincinnati, Philadelphia, St. Louis, and Boston. Others were unable to hold their teams: Hartford, Brooklyn, and Louisville.

The National League now consists of 16 teams, which have been divided into three divisions since 1994. Its newest franchises are located in places like Arizona and Colorado, which weren't even part of the union when the league was founded.

Today, the National League is experiencing a stadium explosion. Only three National League teams play in stadiums built prior to 1993. Ten new National League parks have been opened since 2000, including Citizen's Bank Park in Philadelphia; PETCO Park in San Diego, which opened their doors in 2004; the third Busch Stadium in 2006; the new Nationals Park in 2008; and the most recent—Citi Field—in 2009.

Left: Panorama of Turner Field as the Atlanta Braves play a night game in April 1997.
Joseph Sohm; ChromoSohm Inc./Corbis

NATIONAL LEAGUE EAST

The National League East is a division that has seen massive changes in the last five years. The pre-turn-of-the-century teams, the Braves and the Phillies, play in brand-new, highly regarded ballparks. Of the others, the Mets have a new stadium, Citi Field; the newly arrived Nationals have purpose-built Nationals Park; and the Marlins moved into a new stadium in 2012.

Two stadiums in the National League East Division were built for Olympics. Another was built for football. Montreal's Le Stade Olympique was constructed for the 1976 Summer Olympics, and converted for the Expos the following year. The result was an oversized, clumsy park that never felt quite right for baseball. Little surprise that the franchise moved to Washington in 2005.

Twenty years later, the Braves learned from the Expos' mistakes. Atlanta's stadium for the 1996 Summer Games was specially designed to transform into a baseball friendly park, although the Braves intend to leave it in 2017.

Miami's Marlins Park is the most recent of the ballparks in the national League East, located on the old Miami Orange Bowl site.

New York's Shea Stadium was built for baseball, though it was also enlisted for football,

concerts, boxing matches, and religious events. It, too, was superseded by a new ballpark which opened in 2009.

Shea Stadium at dusk during the National League game between the Philadelphia Phillies and the New York Mets on July 13, 2003.
Photo by Jerry Driendl/Getty Images

ATLANTA BRAVES

TURNER FIELD

ATLANTA BRAVES

Aka: Centennial Olympic Stadium (1996)
Address:
755 Hank Aaron Drive
Atlanta, GA 30315
Capacity: 49,793
Opening day: April 4, 1997—Atlanta Braves 5,
Chicago Cubs 4
Cost to construct: $242.5 million
Architect: Atlanta Stadium Design Team
Dimensions (ft):
Left Field—335
Left Center—380
Center Field—401
Right Center—390
Right Field—330
Defining feature: 100 foot-high replica of Hank
Aaron's 715 HR ball
World Series: 1999
All Star Game: 2000

Memorable moments:
1996 July 19—Muhammad Ali lights the Olympic flame
   atop the stadium that would become Turner Field.
1997 May 16—Michael Tucker breaks up a no-hitter by
   the Cardinals Alan Benes with two outs in bottom
   of ninth. Braves go on to win 1–0 in 13 innings.
1999 September 23—Chipper Jones hits his fourth
   home run in three games to complete a three-
   game sweep over division rival Mets.
1999 October 19—Andruw Jones draws an 11th-
   inning, bases-loaded walk to give the Braves a
   10–9 victory over the Mets and their fifth
   National League pennant of the decade.
1999 October 23—The Braves lose the first game of
   the World Series 4–1 to the Yankees who go on
   to sweep the title 4–0.
2005—The Braves win (90–72) the Eastern Division
   title for the fourteenth consecutive time,
   1991–2005.

Turner Field was born an 85,000-seat, Olympic-sized track and field coliseum.

The Olympics came to Atlanta in 1996, just as the Braves were itching for a new home after playing for three decades in oversized Atlanta-Fulton County Stadium. In a confluence of creativity and good timing, the Braves and the city struck a deal.

The city built a $207 million Olympic stadium in the parking lot of the Braves' old home. (In 1997, the old stadium was imploded, and is now a parking lot for the new.) Athletes from around the world paraded through the facility. Muhammad Ali lit the opening flame. When the Olympians went home, the Braves spent another $35 million to turn the mega-sports complex into a baseball-only facility.

The grandstands were ripped down and 35,000 seats were removed. Dugouts emerged from underneath Olympic bleachers. The Braves locker room was built in what was originally a basement TV studio. The final product was a state-of-the-art, designer ballpark. It is more symmetric than the retro-parks now in fashion. But it offers intimate confines, seats angled toward home plate, and a brick and limestone facade reminiscent of Camden Yards.

Turner Field is not as old-fashioned looking as the other instant classics in Baltimore, Cleveland, or Pittsburgh, though it makes frequent gestures to Braves' history. Seats are decorated with a silhouette of Hank Aaron, whom many locals said the stadium should have been named after, rather than team owner Ted Turner.

It takes a close look to detect the stadium's Olympic lineage. One clue is the unusual outfield, where center and left field are curved, like stadiums built in the 1960s, a holdover from the oval-shaped Olympic Stadium, while the right field fence is a straight line consistent with today's old-style parks.

Outside the stadium, the tall posts that surround Monument Grove—a collection of statues which includes Hank Aaron, Warren Spahn, Eddie Matthews, Phil Niekro, Dale Murphy, and Georgia native Ty Cobb—are the very columns that supported the Olympic Stadium bleachers.

Off the field, the Braves' home resembles a theme park as much as a ballpark. Games, concessions (including food to reflect the visiting team, such as cheesesteaks when the Phillies are in town), and television monitors are ubiquitous. Near a Hall of Fame museum there is a video wall with televisions showing every major-league game in progress. The first fan who catches a home run in a far-away section in the third tier of left field has been promised $1 million, something that baseball experts and those who understand physics agree is unlikely to ever happen.

It was something of a shock in November 2013 when it was announced that the Braves would not be renewing their lease and would leave the Ted for a new ballpark in Cobb County in 2017. Newer than fourteen of the other MLB ballparks, Atlanta mayor Kasim Reed announced that the Ted will be imploded once the Braves leave.

Right: 1999 view of
Turner Field.
*National Baseball Hall of
Fame*

Left: Turner Field in 1999. The notional capacity of around 50,000 has not been neared recently: midway through the 2014 season the average attendance is some 28,000.
National Baseball Hall of Fame

Right: Compare this 2013 view with the 1999 photo at left: not much outward difference although there were significant renovations in 2005. Hidden just behind the out-of-town scoreboard (under the Delta sign) are two Turner Field icons: an enormous Coke bottle and the Chick-Fil-A cow, added in 2008—the local Press thought it "udderly" unique.
Zpb52 via Wikicommons

Below Right: Javy Lopez—#8 of the Atlanta Braves—flies out to left fielder Miguel Cabrera of the Florida Marlins in the seventh inning of the game on July 23, 2003, at Turner Field. The Marlins defeated the Braves in 12 innings 5–4. The scoreboard was replaced in 2005 with a $10 million HD display, then the world's largest.
Photo by Jamie Squire/Getty Images

Right: Kenny Lofton—#7 of the Chicago Cubs—bats against the Atlanta Braves in the second inning of the National League Divisional Series Game 2 on October 1, 2003 at Turner Field. The Braves defeated the Cubs 5–3.
Photo by Craig Jones/Getty Images

Far Right: Construction began in 1964 on a structure that needed to be open in time to receive the Milwaukee Braves who were scheduled to move to Atlanta in time to play on Opening Day 1966. Astonishingly, construction was completed a year early. After Hank Aaron hit his 500th homerun there on July 14, 1968, the park was sometimes referred to as the "House that Hank Built," a not so subtle reference to another ballpark made famous by the balls that George Herman Ruth hit out of it.
National Baseball Hall of Fame

ATLANTA-FULTON COUNTY STADIUM (1966–96)

Home of the Atlanta Braves

The home of Braves was built in less than a year, which was part of what lured the team from its home in Milwaukee. Enclosed, symmetrical and modern, it was known as a place to hit home runs. The power of the park was enhanced by its elevation 1,000 feet above sea level, not as thin-aired as the mile high environs of Denver, but giving batters a few extra feet on long fly balls. The stadium's most famous home run came on opening day, April 8, 1974, when Hank Aaron hit No. 715 over the left field wall, sending him on a well photographed, round-the-bases trot into baseball immortality. The stadium served admirably for 30 years, hosting four World Series in the 1990s, as the once-woeful Braves became the team of the decade. The stadium's final game was a 1 to 0 loss to the New York Yankees in the 1996 World Series.

MIAMI MARLINS

MARLINS PARK

MIAMI MARLINS

Address:
51 Marlins Way
Miami, Florida
Capacity: 36,742
Opening day: April 4, 2012—Florida Marlins 1,
St Louis Cardinals 4
Cost to construct: $634 million
Architect: Populous
Dimensions (ft):
Left Field—344
Left Center—420
Center Field—418
Right Center—392
Right Field—335
Defining feature: That roof.
World Series: None
All-Star Game: None

Memorable moments:
2012 April 12—First win at Marlins Park of the new
season, 5–4 in the 11th against the Astros (a
scoreline repeated on April 15).
2012 May 30—Victory over the Nats gives the Marlins
a 21-win May, a franchise record. At 29–22 the
season could go both ways ... unfortunately it was
downwards and the Marlins ended the season at
the bottom of the National League East.

"Pick up the park and move it 500 miles north, and you've got a real winner," wrote ESPN columnist Jeff Merron about the stadium the Marlins started with. And soon after the Marlins were created, the owners were already looking for ways to let them play under a retractable dome, either in downtown Miami, or at Pro Player.

The heat didn't stop the new franchise gaining immediate success. The Marlins won their first game on April 5, 1993: five years later they won their first World Series. Five years later, they won again, beating the Yankees in six games.

No matter the success, the Marlins needed a roof to protect fans and players from the regular rains and the high temperatures. It cost over $600 million to achieve the stadium controversial owner Jeffrey Loria wanted, but by 2012 there it was, risen like a phoenix from the ashes of the Miami Orange Bowl. Above the 37,000-capacity crowd (the team has moved from the largest stadium in baseball to the smallest) runs MLB's fifth retractable roof. It is formed from three metal-decked operable panels, the center panel at the highest elevation with 200 feet clear over second base to allow for "pop-flies." The 338,000 square feet of roof surface area—some 19 million pounds—can open or close within 13 minutes, traveling at a speed of 39 feet per minute. Average game temperatures have dropped from 85°F to 75°F.

The Orange Bowl is remembered in the Marlins Park East Plaza where a series of art pieces form David Arsham's "Orange Bowl Tribute" which shows what the letters of "MIAMI ORANGE BOWL" would have looked like if they had fallen from their location in the previous facility.

As you look through the huge window towards downtown Miami, your eye is drawn to a bizarre, multicolored edifice behind the outfield fence in left-centerfield. After a Marlin home run the colorful, $2.5 million, 75ft tall structure provides moving waves along the bottom and spins marlins, seagulls and flamingos. Is the new stadium a bizarre misjudgment or a brilliant coup? The jury's still out.

Above and Right: The field at Marlins Park with the Miami skyline in the background. In left centerfield is the Marlinator (detail above) that animates should the Marlins hit a home run The Marlins Park design also provides an open East end to provide unobstructed views to the Downtown Miami Skyline.
Dan Lundberg via Wikicommons

Left and Below Two views of the then Pro Player Stadium. Built by Wayne Huizenga after he had bought the Miami Dolphins, it cost $10 million to renovate it for baseball. In 1996 Pro Player, a division of Fruit-of-the-Loom, bought the naming rights to the stadium.
Digitalballparks.com

Right: An night exterior view of Pro Player Stadium.
Digitalballparks.com

SUN LIFE STADIUM (1993–2011)
Home of the Florida Marlins

Built for football, it took some doing—and about $10 million—to make it compatible for baseball, the first football stadium to be so converted. A hydraulically operated pitcher's mound was installed, a new press box for baseball media was added, and baseball locker rooms built. Due to its football-sized dimensions, huge numbers of empty orange seats, trimmed in teal and blue, made for a colorful but empty appearance. The Marlins decided to close the upper deck with blue tarps, limiting capacity and lending the park a more intimate feel. The entrance to the park, surrounded by pastel colors and palm trees, was unmistakably Florida. So is the weather, which often makes it uncomfortably hot during day games and thunderstorming at night.

Originally built as the John Robbie Stadium in 1987, the facility enjoyed many other names— Pro Player Park (or Stadium) in 1996–2005, Dolphin (or Dolphins) Stadium 2005–09, Land Shar Stadium 2009–10, and finally from 2010, Sun Life Stadium.

From the start the stadium saw a remarkable amount of post-season excitement. In 1997, the Marlins stunned the baseball world by winning the World Series in seven games over the Cleveland Indians. Attendance suffered when the old owners sold off the team's best talent, but a new crop of Marlins repeated the triumph in 2003 with a surprise six-game World Series victory over the New York Yankees. The success led to a new stadium and Sun Life reverted to football full-time.

NEW YORK METS

CITI FIELD

NEW YORK

Address:
Roosevelt Avenue, Flushing.
Queens, NY 11354
Capacity: 41,922 (more with standing room)
Opening day: April 13, 2009—San Diego Padres 6,
New York Mets 5
Cost to construct: $900 million
Architect: Populous
Dimensions (ft):
Left Field—335
Left Center—364
Center Field—408
Right Center—378
Right Field—330
Defining feature: Noisy jets flying in and out of La
Guardia. The Mets Magic Top Hat with its red apple
rising out when a Mets' player hits a homer has been
replicated in the new stadium.
World Series: None
All-Star Game: 2013

Memorable moments:
2009 March 29—First game played at Citi Field, a
 college game between St. John's and Georgetown.
2009 April 3—The Mets play their first game at Citi
 Field, an exhibition game against the Boston Red
 Sox.
2009 April 13—Jody Gerut becomes the first player in
 MLB history to open a ballpark with a home run.
2009 April 15—The Mets beat the Padres 7–2 for their
 first win at Citi Field.
2009 April 17—Gary Sheffield hits his 500th home run
 against the Milwaukee Brewers.
2009 July—Paul McCartney performs three sold-out
 concerts at Citi Field.
2011 August 15—Against the Padres in a 5–4 win
 Jason Isringhausen becomes the 23rd pitcher to
 record 300 career saves.
2012 June 1—Johan Setana records the first no-hitter
 in Mets' history, against the Cardinals in an 8–0
 win.

The Mets have been playing in the National League's Eastern Division since 1969. They entered the league as an expansion team in 1962 and played at the old Polo Grounds. Even though managed by the legendary Casey Stengel, the Mets were easily one of the worst teams in history. They made their swansong at the Polo Grounds on September 18, 1963, and transferred to the new Shea Stadium in 1964.

Few parks in baseball possessed so many memories and so little soul as Shea. Opened in an era of cookie-cutter parks, Shea's builders boasted of its symmetrical geometry, its grand four-story escalator system, its tall ramps, its tidy four-tier layout, and its lack of view-blocking pillars. It was the first stadium built able to make a rapid transition to football, and one of the first to feature a novel "color" scoreboard.

It was a wonder in a time gone by. Today, its most remarkable feature is its noise, which has nothing to do with its fans, but the stadium's unfortunate location in the flight path of New York La Guardia Airport, which averages more than 1,000 flights a day. The disrupting engine roar, which has prompted some players to wear earplugs, is a constant reminder that this is not a quaint ball yard. The stadium, originally to be called Flushing Meadows Park, was instead named after the lawyer who led the effort to bring the Mets to New York, returning National League baseball to New York after the departure of the Dodgers and the Giants in 1957.

William Alfred Shea christened the stadium with two bottles of water—one from the water near Ebbets Field, the Dodgers' old home, and one from the Harlem River near the Polo Grounds, where the Giants had played (and the Mets spent their first two seasons.)

As bad as the Mets were at the beginning, they turned things around in a big way in 1969. That year, the "Miracle Mets" came from far behind to catch the Cubs late in the season, knocked off the Braves in the playoffs, then stunned the favored Baltimore Orioles in the World Series 4–1. The team returned to baseball's championship in 1973, 1986, and 2000. In 1986 they defeated the Red Sox in seven games, but they lost crosstown series to the Yankees in 1973 and 2000.

They left Shea Stadium for the new Citi Field at the end of the 2008 season. Named after the Citigroup financial service company, it is only a few yards away from Shea, built on one of its parking lots. Citi Field has a retro feel to it. Designed by the then HOK Sport, the exterior is clad in traditional materials such as limestone, granite, cast stone, and brick—the latter's color a close match to that used at Brooklyn's old Ebbets Field. Arches add to the retro feel. The front entrance features a rotunda named after Brooklyn Dodgers legend Jackie Robinson. The field will make a fine home for the Mets for years to come.

Right: Citi Field's irregular outfield dimensions, classical façade, and intimate seating bowl are reminiscent of baseball's old ballparks, while the high-tech scoreboards, comfortable seats, and ample amenities provide the ultimate in modern conveniences. *Rob Tringali/ Sportschrome/Getty Images*

Above: The granite, limestone, and brick exterior of Citi Field, along with the arched windows and gates are inspired by the design of Brooklyn's Ebbets Field and other classic ballparks of an earlier era. 2009. *Al Bello/Getty Images*

Left: In an era of cookie-cutter parks, Shea Stadium was distinctive not for its architectural features, but for its location below the flight path of New York's La Guardia airport With an average of 1,000 a day, even the players sometimes wore earplugs.
National Baseball Hall of Fame

Right: Shea Stadium from the upper deck during the game between the Philadelphia Phillies and the New York Mets on July 13, 2003. The Mets won 4–3. The stadium had been designed to be expanded. However, when plans were drawn up to add seats but cover the stadium with a dome, they had to be scrapped because the engineers said the stadium could collapse under the weight. *Photo by Jerry Driendl/Getty Images*

PHILADELPHIA PHILLIES

CITIZENS BANK PARK

PHILADELPHIA PHILLIES

Address: Pattison Avenue, Philadelphia
Capacity: 43,651
Opening Day: April 12, 2004. Cincinnati Reds 4, Philadelphia Phillies 1
Cost to construct: $346 million
Architect: Ewing Cole Cherry Brott (ECCB) and HOK
Dimensions (ft):
Left Field—329
Left Center—370
Center Field—401
Right Center—370
Right Field—330
Defining feature: Electronic Liberty Bell set off by home run
World Series: 2008, 2009
All-Star Game: None

Memorable moments:
2004 April 12—Bobby Abreu of the Phillies hit the ballpark's first home run.
2008 October 25—The Phillies defeat the Tampa Bay Rays, 5–4 in Game 3. of the World Series
2008 October 29—The suspended Game Five (caused torrential rain) is resumed and the Phillies defeat the Rays, 4–3, thus gaining their second World Series victory. A record crowd of 45,940 watch.
2009 October 21—by beating the Dodgers 10–4 to win the National League Championship, the Phillies advance to the World Series to defend their 2008 title. 46,214 watch.
2009 November 2—The Phillies win Game 5 of the World Series against the Yankees 8–6 but go on to lose the next game 7–3 and the series 4–2.

Philadelphia has had the best of ballparks, and the worst of ballparks. Now it has a relatively new one. Citizens Bank Park, opened in time for the 2004 season, is Philadelphia's edition of a throwback park, said to mimic stately Shibe Park, which was opened before World War I, and Baker Bowl, where the Phillies began playing baseball in the time of Mark Twain.

It is located across the street from Veterans Stadium, the run down cookie-cutter arena where the Phillies spent the last 30 years. The new park was tilted 45 degrees clockwise, in order to frame a panorama of downtown Philadelphia over its center-field wall. It has a natural grass infield and dirt basepaths, as compared to the artificial turf and small sliding pits in the Vet. It contains 20,000 fewer seats, and a concourse that allows fans to watch the action while they are walking around. The seats behind the plate are 10 feet closer than at the old stadium, and about half the seats are located below the concourse.

The outfield was loosely modeled after Shibe Park, which was best remembered for its enormous French Renaissance facade. Red steel, brick, and stone give the exterior a classic feel, and its main entrances are framed by light standards for a grand approach. Rising 50 feet above first, home, and third are glass towers which are illuminated at night.

The field's distinctive shape, with a little lip in left field, is expected to create entertaining bounces. The architects conducted extensive wind studies, measuring ball trajectories and wind velocities which led them to conclude that Citizens Bank Park will be neither a hitter's nor a pitcher's park.

The center-field concession area is dedicated to Philly Hall of Famer and broadcaster Richie Ashburn. Greg "the Bull" Luzinski, who enjoyed many years of glory at the Vet, serves BBQ in Ashburn Alley, as Boog Powell does for Oriole fans at Baltimore's Camden Yards.

A statue of Connie Mack, the great Philadelphia A's player and manager has been brought over from the Vet. And inside the park, bronze statues honoring Phillies legends Mike Schmidt, Steve Carlton, Robin Roberts and Richie Ashburn celebrate the Phillies' past. A lot of emotional farewells were paid to the Vet in its final days, but the field at Citizens Bank Park was declared ready to go after the 2003 season amid high expectations—expectations that were justified within five years when the Phillies advanced to and won the 2008 World Series. The next year they reached the World Series again but failed narrowly to record back-to-back victories losing to the Yankees.

Considered one of the most hitter-friendly ballparks in MLB, in 2009 it saw 149 home runs, the most in the National League and second in the majors behind only the new Yankee Stadium that was goinng through an equally purple period. This certainly brought in the crowds—as did the Phillies' excellent form—and that year the team set an all-time attendance record for the stadium, attracting more than 3.5 million fans.

Right: Philadelphia Phillies pitcher Randy Wolf delivers the first pitch to Cincinatti Reds D'Angelo Jiminez in the new Citizens Bank Ballpark, April 12, 2004.
© Tim Shaffer/Reuters/Corbis

Far Left: The Phillies had played baseball in "The Vet" for thirty-two years when it finally closed at the end of the 2003 season. Players and fans alike were ready to move on. The once-great stadium had seen its best days many years ago.
National Baseball Hall of Fame

Left: The Vet's unique rounded rectangular shape has been the setting for two All-Star Games (1976, 1996) and three World Series (1980, 1983, and 1993).
National Baseball Hall of Fame

SHIBE PARK (1909–70)

Home of the Philadelphia Athletics 1909–54
Home of the Philadelphia Phillies 1938–70

Just as Baltimore's Camden Yards would do eight decades later, Shibe Park touched off a baseball revolution. Steel-and-concrete, aesthetically pleasing, huge, and with attention to detail, the home of the Philadelphia Athletics and then the Phillies was widely imitated. Over the next five years, Ebbets Field, Forbes Field, Wrigley Field, Fenway Park, Braves Field, and Comiskey Park all opened, while still others were redone in concrete and steel. Beyond its distinctive field and enormous confines, Shibe was distinguished by its enormous French Renaissance façade that belied the notion that it was a mere ballpark.

Named in honor of the A's owner Ben Shibe, it was renamed Connie Mack Stadium in 1953. In 1971 the Phillies moved to Veterans Stadium, a park then hailed as modern, built in the mold of parks in St. Louis, Cincinnati and Pittsburgh. By the time of its last game in 2003, it was ridiculed as sterile and among baseball's worst parks.

Far Left: Hall of Famers who wore a Phillies uniform and played at The Vet include Mike Schmidt, Joe Morgan, Tony Perez, and Steve Carlton.
National Baseball Hall of Fame

Left: Roy Campanella (C) scoring during the Dodgers-Phillies game of October 1, 1949 at Shibe Park.
Photo by George Silk//Time Life Pictures via Getty Images

WASHINGTON NATIONALS

NATIONALS PARK

WASHINGTON NATIONALS

Address:
1500 South Capitol Street, SE
Washington, D.C. 20003
Capacity: 41,888
Opening day: March 30, 2008—Atlanta Braves 2, Washington Nationals 3
Cost to construct: $611 million
Architect: Populous
Dimensions (ft):
Left Field—336
Left Center—377
Center Field—402
Right Center—370
Right Field—335
Defining feature: A grove of cherry blossoms located just beyond the left field bleachers.
World Series: None
All-Star Game: None

Memorable moments:
2008 March 22—The George Washington University Colonials play the first game in Nationals Park defeating Saint Joseph's University 9–4.
2008 March 30—President George W. Bush threw the ceremonial first pitch to Nationals' manager Manny Acta.
2008 April 17—Pope Benedict XVI celebrated Mass at Nationals Park for 47,000 people.
2009 June 4—SF Giants' Randy Johnson becomes the 24th pitcher in MLB history to reach 300 wins.
2009 July 4—Nats' Adam Dunn becomes the 123rd player to hit 300 career home runs.
2009 July 27—Josh Willingham hits two grand slams in a game against the Milwaukee Brewers, only the 13th player in MLB history to do this.
2009 October 4—Victory in their final game gives the Nats the unusual honor of being the only team in MLB history to start a season with seven losses and end with seven wins.

When the American League transformed itself into a major league in 1901, the powers-that-be decided that the fledgling league needed a major presence on the East Coast, so in 1900 the Kansas City team moved to the capital and became the Washington Nationals or "Nats," more commonly known as the Senators.

Under the leadership of manager—and later owner—Clark Griffith, the Nats took the American League Championship in 1924 and 1925. One more title came in 1933, but over the next twenty-six years the Nats were destined to have just four more winning seasons. Griffith died in October 1955 and his son, Calvin, took over. He became convinced that a move was in the team's best interest, and after 1960 they moved to Minnesota and became the Twins.

The capital was not left without a major league baseball team because a new expansion Washington Senators debuted for the 1961 season. They, too, played at Griffith Stadium, but stayed for just one season, moving to the new D.C. Stadium, one of the first multipurpose "cookie cutter" stadiums, playing their first game there on April 9, 1962. In 1968 the facility was renamed RFK Stadium in honor of the assassinated Attorney General Robert F. Kennedy. The Senators shared the stadium, with the NFL's Washington Redskins, which used RFK until they moved into their own new FedEx Field in 1996.

The Senators were not a good baseball team. In their first four seasons they hit the century mark in losses and they used up five managers in just a decade. Financial problems and a dwindling fan base soon brought an end to the second Senators and 71 years of continuous major league baseball in the capital. They played their last gameat RFK Stadium on September 30, 1971. The franchise moved to the Dallas-Fort Worth area and became the Texas Rangers.

It took more than three decades to bring baseball back to the nation's capital, but diehard fans were rewarded in 2005, when the former Montreal Expos made their home debut on April 15 as the reincarnated Washington Nationals. The Expos/ Nationals had taken a bizarre route to the Capital—including an aborted MLB plan to kill the franchise, and a stint playing part-time in Puerto Rico—but Washington fans enthusiastically welcomed the team. The city invested more the $18.5 million upgrading RFK for baseball, and also agreed to build a new $535 million baseball-only stadium. After considerable political wrangling a site was selected at South Capitol and N streets SE, and the stadium—Nationals Park—opened for the 2008 season. The first sports facility in the U.S. to be Leadership in Energy and Environmental Design certified, it is a contemporary design with half of its seats on the lower deck nearer the action.

Right: Nationals Park at twilight during their first home game in Washington, March 29, 2008. *Jason Reed/Reuters/Corbis*

Overleaf: Panorama of Nationals Stadium during the Nationals vs. Rangers game of June 22, 2008. *Brian Williams*

Left: A fisheye view of Washington Nationals game against the Cincinnati Reds on August 25, 2005, at RFK Stadium. The Reds defeated the Nationals 5–3. *MLB Photos via Getty Images*

NATIONAL LEAGUE CENTRAL

The teams of the National League Central are among baseball's oldest. Baseball has been played in Chicago, Cincinnati, Pittsburgh, and St. Louis since the 19th century. However, the division's ballparks are among the game's newest.

Chicago's Wrigley Field, opened in 1916, is the National League's oldest park, and in the eyes of many purists, baseball's best. The manual scoreboard, outfield wall ivy, and close confines have come to define the game. Seventy-five years after Wrigley was built, four National League Central division teams opened 21st century parks.

The Houston Astros replaced their fully enclosed Astrodome with a downtown, retractable-dome stadium in 2000 and then—after 51 seasons in the National League—decamped to the American League West in 2013. Pittsburgh moved into a new ball yard on the banks of the Allegheny River that some claim is every bit as pleasant as Wrigley. Milwaukee also opened a new park in 2001, replacing County Stadium, while Cincinnati moved from sterile Riverfront Stadium, later named Cinergy Field, to a new home in 2003. Not to be outdone, the St. Louis Cardinals built a new stadium (the third Busch Stadium) in time for the 2006 season, leaving Wrigley Field as the division's only 20th century park.

Right: View of the Great American Ball Park from home plate upper level during the game between the Cincinnati Reds and the Houston Astros.
Photo by Jerry Driendl/Getty Images

CHICAGO CUBS

WRIGLEY FIELD

CHICAGO CUBS

Aka: Weeghman Park (1914–15), Cubs Park (1916–26)
Address:
1060 West Addison
Chicago, IL 60613
Capacity: 41,072
Opening day: April 23, 1914—Chicago Federals 9, Kansas City Packers 1
Opening day: (Cubs) April 20, 1916—Chicago Cubs 7, Cincinnati Reds 6 (11 innings)
Cost to construct: $250,000
Architect: Zachary Taylor Davis
Dimensions (ft):
Left Field—355
Left Center—368
Center Field—400
Right Center—368
Right Field—353
Defining feature: Outfield ivy
Little-known ground rule: Baseball stuck in vines covering bleacher wall: Double
World Series: 1918, 1929, 1932, 1935, 1938, 1945
All-Star Game: 1947, 1962, 1990

Memorable moments:
1922 August 25—Cubs beat Phillies 26–23 in Major League Baseball's highest scoring game.
1932 October 1—Babe Ruth gestures toward the center field bleachers in game three of the World Series before hitting the ball there for his second homer.
1938 September 28—Gabby Hartnett's "Homer in the Gloamin" gives the Cubs their third consecutive National League pennant.
1945—The Cubs' last appearance in the World Series in 65 years, the longest drought in the majors.
1998 September 13—Sammy Sosa hits home run #62 to eclipse Roger Maris' single-season record.
2003 October 14—With the Cubs leading 3–0 and just five outs from a first World Series in 58 years, a fan reaches for a foul ball and deprives left fielder Moises Alou a chance to make a catch. The Marlins go on to score eight runs and win the pennant.

Wrigley Field is what every baseball park wants to be.

Simple, intimate, handsome, and distinct, cities and team owners around the country have spent hundreds of millions of dollars, hired architects, engineers, and historians, all hoping to recreate what has existed on Chicago's North side for nearly a century.

Built on the grounds of a seminary in 1914, the park opened as Weeghman Park, home to the Chicago Federals (also known as the Whales) in the soon-to-be defunct Federal League. Two years later it was Cubs Park, when the National League team moved in, and then Wrigley Field when the chewing gum magnate took control of the team a decade later.

Change marked Wrigley's early years. A second deck was added in 1927. The signature bleachers and 27-foot high scoreboard were built in 1937. That same year, Bill Veeck planted hundreds of Boston Ivy plants along the outfield brick wall. A clock was added atop the scoreboard four years later. Since then, time has essentially stood still inside the "friendly confines" which Hack Wilson, Ernie Banks, Billy Williams, Fergie Jenkins, Ryne Sandberg, and Sammy Sosa have all called home.

Take a look at a picture of Wrigley in the early 1940s and another from today. The top hats and black jackets have been replaced by bright blue Cubbie caps and t-shirts and the high rises beyond center field have grown taller, but little else has changed. There were no billboards inside the park then, and there are none today. The scoreboard is still hand-operated (and not large enough to accommodate every out-of-town game since the major leagues expanded.) After each Cub victory, a white flag with a blue W is raised high above the scoreboard, a white L on a blue flag indicates a loss, a system originally created to let Wrigley's neighbors keep track of their team long before the advent of sports tickers or ESPN.

Chicago baseball in the 21st century is much as it was prior to World War II, providing an incredible link to another era and one that ballparks from Baltimore to Seattle have tried to capture for themselves.

Wrigley Field, as the second oldest major-league park after Fenway, is the birthplace of many baseball traditions. It was the first place that allowed fans to keep balls hit into the stands. The first concession stands were built in the park's opening year, after patrons complained that roaming vendors were blocking their view. In 1941, the Cubs became the first team to play organ music in its ballpark. It is here that Harry Caray, leaning outside his broadcast booth with microphone in hand and beer poorly concealed behind the window, made famous the tradition of singing *Take Me Out To The Ballgame* during the seventh inning stretch which is now imitated wherever baseball is played.

Until 1988, Wrigley's most distinctive feature was its lack of lights. Team owners were ready to install them in time for the 1942 season when the U.S. was attacked at Pearl Harbor. The day after the attack, team owner P.K. Wrigley donated the equipment to the War Department. Lights were finally erected in 1988 after league officials threatened to hold Cubs postseason games at the home of the rival Cardinals in St. Louis.

Wrigley's first night game, in what some saw as an omen, was suspended in the fourth inning after a torrential downpour. The first official game was played the following night when the Cubs beat the Mets 6 to 4.

After thousands of games, no baseball has yet hit the center-field scoreboard, though a towering home run hit onto Sheffield Avenue by Bill Nicholson in 1948, and another one hit onto Waveland Avenue in 1959 by Roberto Clemente, barely missed. Sam Snead reached the scoreboard with a golf ball, prior to a game in 1951.

Cub fans are familiar with many smaller changes over the years. Luxury boxes have been added to bring in revenue, and in 1970 a basket was installed along the bleachers to keep fans from interfering with balls. Seats have been erected on the rooftops along Waveland and Sheffield Avenues, where more casual viewing was once a tradition.

Yet Wrigley baseball looks much the same today as it did when Zip Zabel came in to pitch 18 innings in relief over Brooklyn in 1915, when Stan Musial collected his 3,000 hit, when Ernie Banks hit his 512th and final home run, when Fergie Jenkins pitched his 3,000 strikeout, and when Pete Rose tied Ty Cobb with hit No. 4,191.

For all Wrigley has witnessed, it has never seen a Cubs World Series celebration. As one of the league's most dominant teams in the first half of the 20th century, the Cubs brought the World Series to Wrigley six times between 1918 and 1945, losing each time. The Cubs' last championship team was in 1908, well before there was a ballpark at the corner of Addison and Sheffield.

Above: An undated photo showing Wrigley prior to the 1937 season when its signature bleachers were constructed. The alterations and enhancements made it one of the most pleasant places on earth to watch a ballgame.
National Baseball Hall of Fame

Left: Exterior view of Wrigley Field during the game between the Philadelphia Phillies and the Chicago Cubs on July 23, 2003.
Photo by Jerry Driendl/Getty Images

Above: Wrigley Field from a right field skybox across the street from the ballpark during the game between the Phillies and the Cubs on July 23, 2003.
Photo by Jerry Driendl/Getty Images

Right: An aerial view of Wrigley Field. Easy to see why even the players refer to this classic park as the "Friendly Confines." By the time this photo was taken the bleachers and a second level of seats had been added to meet the fan demand.
National Baseball Hall of Fame

Right: Wrigley Field's center-field scoreboard during the game between the Phillies and the Cubs on July 23, 2003. *Photo by Jerry Driendl/Getty Images*

Inset: The ivy and scoreboard were introduced to Wrigley Field by Bill Veeck in 1937 It is one of the last hand-turned scoreboards (there's one at Fenway, too) and as the ground has been listed as a National Landmark, changes are unlikely. *National Baseball Hall of Fame*

Right: A packed Wrigley Field seen from the left-field stands.
Digitalballparks.com

Far Right: The Florida Marlins celebrate their 9–6 win over the Chicago Cubs during game seven of the National League Championship series October 15, 2003.
Brian Bahr/Getty Images

Far Right, Inset: Cubs' bleacher band, seen at Wrigley Field.
Digitalballparks.com

Right: A good view of the ivy, the scoreboard, and the North Sheffield Avenue seating.
Digitalballparks.com

CINCINNATI REDS

GREAT AMERICAN BALLPARK

CINCINNATI REDS

Address:
100 Main Street
Cincinnati, Ohio 45202.
Capacity: 42,059
Opening day: March 31, 2003—Pittsburgh Pirates 10, Cincinnati Reds 1
Cost to construct: $290 million
Architect: HOK Sports
Dimensions (ft):
Left Field—328
Left Center—379
Center Field—404
Right Center—370
Right Field—325
Defining feature: "The Gap" in seats down the left field line
Most expensive seat: $225
Cheapest seat: $5
World Series: None
All-Star Game: chosen for 2015

Memorable moments:
2003 March 31—Former President George Bush, filling in for his son, President George W. Bush, throws out the ceremonial first pitch on the park's opening day.
2003 April 4—Sammy Sosa hits his 500th home run.
2003 July 21—Russell Branyan hits the stadium's first grand slam.
2004 September 25—Cincinnati Reds Hall of Fame opens next to Great American Ball Park.
2006 April 3—President George Bush becomes the first sitting president to throw out the first pitch at a Reds game.
2008 June 8—Ken Griffey, Jr. hits his 600th home run.
2010 October 10—First postseason game in the GABP sees the Phillies shutout the Reds 2–0.
2013 July 2—The first no-hitter at the GABP, by Reds' pitcher Homer Bailey.

Professional baseball began in Cincinnati. From the Union Cricket Club Grounds, where the Cincinnati Red Stockings first played in 1869, the Bank Street Grounds, where ladies had their own entrance, Crosley Field, where baseball had its first night game, to Riverfront Stadium where Hank Aaron tied Babe Ruth for the all-time home run record and Pete Rose passed Ty Cobb for baseball's all-time hit lead, the city on the banks of the Ohio River has always been a baseball town.

Cincinnati's latest park, opened in 2003, hopes to play off the tradition. The scoreboard clock is a replica of the one that once sat in Crosley Field. The main entry and even the seats were designed to resemble the old park. A rose garden is being grown outside the stadium itself, on the very spot where Pete Rose's record 4,192nd hit landed in old Riverfront Stadium.

At the same time, this is a thoroughly modern park, where season tickets to the cushioned seats just 50 feet from home plate ("closer to the batter than the pitcher," the team boasts) with special access to food and drink, sell for more than some players' annual salaries in baseball's not too distant past.

After sharing a home with the Bengals for 30 years at circular Riverfront Stadium, the Reds new home is built exclusively for baseball. It features an imposing, 68-foot high, 217-foot wide scoreboard, which is one of the major's largest.

The Great American Ballpark's signature feature is "The Gap" down the 3rd base line. The unique break in the seating makes for better angles and proximity to the field for seats down the line, opens up views of downtown for those inside the park, and lets passing pedestrians on the outside catch a glimpse of the field.

The exterior is brick with cast stone and painted steel, intended to reflect the architecture of Cincinnati and the nearby Roebling Suspension Bridge which crosses the Ohio River into Kentucky. Views of the river add to the park's character, but it would take a 580-foot shot to deposit a home run into the water. Among the park's other features is a statue of slugger Ted Kluzinski carry a bat on his shoulder like a lumberjack's ax, and a pair of smokestacks which shoot fireworks when a Reds player homers

The Great American Ballpark has fewer of the "retro" touches featured in new parks in Baltimore, Denver, San Francisco, or Pittsburgh. A panel of six architects shown the stadium by the *Cincinnati Enquirer* a week before it opened ripped the stadium as fragmented, erratic, and failing to provide either continuity or order.

The ballpark's name comes from the Great American Insurance company, which bought the naming rights for 30 years at a price of $75 million.

The only major alteration to the ballpark since construction came in 2009 when Daktronics replaced the scoreboards with new hi-def video displays.

Right: A view of the Great American Ball Park and the Cincinnati skyline during a game between the Astros and the Reds.
Photo by Jerry Driendl/Getty Images

Right: The Great American Ball Park from home plate upper level during a National League game between the Cincinnati Reds and the Houston Astros. In the background the Ohio River flows past the stadium.
Photo by Jerry Driendl/Getty Images

The Great American Ball
Park and the Cincinnati
night skyline. The
suspension bridge is the
Roebling Suspension
Bridge, erected in 1866 as
the Covington and
Cincinnati Bridge and
renamed after its designer
John A. Roebling.
*Photo by Jerry
Driendl/Getty Images*

Above: Aerial view of the then Riverfront Stadium. It would be renamed Cinergy Field in 1996 after Cincinnati's electric company paid $6 million for the privilege.
National Baseball Hall of Fame

Left: Spectators aboard boats floating on the Ohio River watch as Cinergy Field is imploded on December 29, 2002, to make room for the nearby Great American Ballpark (on the right). More than 1,200lb of explosive material was used.
Photo by Mike Simons/Getty Images

MILWAUKEE BREWERS

MILLER PARK

MILWAUKEE BREWERS:

Address:
One Brewers Way
Milwaukee, WI 53214
Capacity: 41,900
Opening Day: April 6, 2001—Milwaukee Brewers 5, Cincinnati Reds 4
Cost to construct: $400 million
Architect: HKS, Inc. (Dallas), NBBJ (L.A.), Eppstein Uhen Architects (Milwaukee)
Dimensions (ft):
Left Field—344
Left Center—370
Center Field—400
Right Center—374
Right Field—345
Defining feature: Bernie Brewer
World Series: None
All-Star Game: 2002

Memorable moments:
2001 April 6—President Bush throws out the ceremonial first pitch, and the Brewers rally behind Richie Sexson's eighth-inning home run to beat the Cincinnati Reds in Miller Park's debut.
2002 May 23—Dodger outfielder Shawn Green hits four home runs, seven RBI, scores six runs and sets a major-league record with 19 total bases.
2003 July 9—Pittsburgh outfielder Randall Simon is lead away in handcuffs after belting a costumed, 19-year-old woman participating in the sixth inning sausage race, with a baseball bat.
2006 July 29—The chorizo joins the bratwurst, the Italian, the Polish, and the hot dog in the sausage race. It will become a full-time member in 2007.
2008—The Brewers hit a new franchise mark for attendance with over three million for the season.
2008 October 4—The first postseason game at Miller Park sees the Brewers beat the Phillies, but the next day Philadelphia win the NLDS 3–1.
2011 October 7—The Brewers beat the Diamondbacks 3–2 for their first playoff series win since 1982.

After playing for 30 years in County Stadium, a ballpark as plain as its name, the Brewers opened the new millennium in a park with all the latest bells and whistles.

Miller Park is the major leagues' latest retractable dome stadium, this one built in a unique fan shape, in which the 12,000-ton roof pivots around a point near home plate, covering more than 10 acres, and able to open and shut in just over 10 minutes.

The convertible structure not only means year-round climate control in a northern climate where April and September are pushing the baseball envelope, it also strikes wonder in the upper Midwest cheeseheads, who shattered attendance records in the park's first year. During the opening season, fans stuck around after the game on nice summer nights to watch the roof close to the symphonic sounds of Johann Strauss' "Blue Danube Waltz."

The stadium took almost five years to build, opening a year late after a tragic crane accident in 1999 killed three steel workers, and added $100 million to the project's cost.

The roof stands more than 30 stories high at its peak, adding an imposing new landmark to Milwaukee's modest skyline. The Brewers claim on their internet site, rather oddly, that the stadium weighs the equivalent of 62.5 million bowling balls, and that it would take 4.66 billion baseballs to fill it top to bottom.

Architects boast that the roof's steel mirrors the bridges over the Menomonee River, though the height of the walls and the omnipresence of the dome has led fans to complain that it feels like an indoor stadium even when the roof is open.

Patrons in County Stadium got to watch the project from their seats, as it was built just beyond centerfield in what was a parking lot. It includes a manual scoreboard and seats close to the field in the vain of other recent parks. Brewer Hall of Famer Robin Yount helped design the park's dimensions, which includes a quirky outfield with unique slants and angles.

Outside is a classic brick facade, with statues of Yount and Hank Aaron.

The Brewers transplanted some of their most distinctive traditions from County Stadium,

including Bernie Brewer, who used to slide down an enormous, several-story high slide into a beer stein, and now does the same onto a platform in left field. Humans dressed in sausage costumes race around the bases in the middle of the sixth inning. And huge parking lots facilitate Wisconsin's obsession with tailgate parties.

Outside, eight names have been immortalized on a "Walk of Fame," that encircles the ballpark plaza, including Aaron, Yount, Rollie Fingers, Cecil Cooper, Paul Molitor, Allan H. (Bud) Selig, Harry Dalton and Bob Uecker.

The stadium offers $1 "Ueker seats," named after the well known Brewer's broadcaster, obstructed by roof pivots and located in the upper deck terrace, but still one of the best deals in baseball.

Right: A view of the entrance to Miller Park before the game between the Milwaukee Brewers and the Cincinnati Reds on May 17, 2003. The Brewers defeated the Reds 8–6.
Photo by Jonathan Daniel/Getty Images

This Page: Miller Park during the game between the Milwaukee Brewers and the Cincinnati Reds on May 17, 2003. The Brewers defeated the Reds 8–6.
Photo by Jonathan Daniel/Getty Images

Opposite, Left: Kazuhiro Sasaki of the Seattle Mariners and his son Shogo take in the media during batting practice for the MLB All-Star Game and MLB All-Star Home Run Derby July 8, 2002, at Miller Park.
Photo by Matthew Stockman/Getty Images

Opposite, Right: Mascot Bernie Brewer of the Milwaukee Brewers looks on from "Bernie's Dugout" during the game against the Cincinnati Reds at Miller Park on May 17, 2003. The Brewers defeated the Reds 8–6.
Photo by Jonathan Daniel/Getty Images

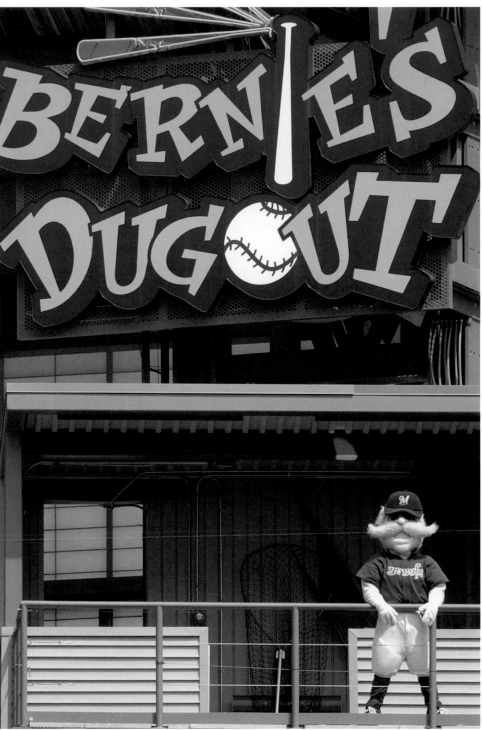

MILWAUKEE COUNTY STADIUM (1953-2000)
Home of the Milwaukee Braves (1953-1965)
Home of the Milwaukee Brewers (1970-2000)

Unless you count the man who slid into a beer stein after each Brewer home run, there were few frills at Milwaukee County Stadium. The straight-forward ballpark was made exclusively for baseball, and the fans who sang "Beer Barrel Polka" during the seventh-inning stretch rarely complained. It is here that Hank Aaron started his remarkable career, and where Warren Spahn enjoyed nine, 20-win seasons.

County Stadium was home to the Braves when they moved from Boston in 1953, and was a National League park for 13 seasons until their departure for Atlanta 13 years later. The American League Brewers moved in before the 1970 season (and 27 years before their return to the National League.)

Left: Milwaukee County Stadium in the 1950s. *Milwaukee Journal/National Baseball Hall of Fame*

Right: Milwaukee County Stadium from behind the right field foul post. *Milwaukee Journal/National Baseball Hall of Fame*

PITTSBURGH PIRATES

PNC PARK

PITTSBURGH PIRATES

Address:
115 Federal Street
Pittsburgh, PA 15212
Capacity: 38,365
Opening day: April 9, 2001—Cincinnati Reds 8, Pittsburgh Pirates 2
Cost to construct: $262 million
Architect: HOK Sports
Dimensions (ft):
Left Field—325
Left Center—389
Center Field—399
Right Center—375
Right Field—320
Defining feature: Roberto Clemente Bridge
World Series: None
All-Star Game: 2006

Memorable moments:
2001 June 27—Pirates Manager Lloyd McClendon steals first base, literally, after being ejected from the game for disputing a call at first base. Play is resumed after a replacement base is located and installed.
2001 July 28—Brian Giles hits a grand slam to cap a two-out, seven-run rally in the bottom of the ninth inning to beat the Astros 9–8.
2002 July 6—Houston's Daryle Ward becomes the first player to hit a home run into the Allegheny River over the park's right field wall, a shot estimated at 479 feet.
2010 April 27—The Pirates break a 22-game losing streak at Miller Park beating the Brewers 7–3.
2013 October 4—After 20 years of losing seasons the Bucs win a postseason game, beating the Cardinals 7–1.

Right: 24 Jun 2001: A general view of the game between the Montreal Expos and the Pittsburgh Pirates at PNC Park. The Expos defeated the Pirates 11–4.
Photo by Rick Stewart/Allsport via Getty Images

The nation's ultimate boutique park is located in its Iron City.

At first glance, PNC Park looks like something out of a child's baseball fantasy. The outfield wall reveals sweeping views of the Allegheny River, the Depression-era Roberto Clemente bridge, river boats, and downtown Pittsburgh. The stadium's simple two-deck construction and limited seating make it perhaps the most intimate park in the major leagues. Old fashioned light standards add to the historic feel, while a huge scoreboard updates every game in baseball. Fans can arrive by riverboat, or by walking across the picturesque suspension bridge from downtown, which is closed to vehicles on game days.

If Camden Yards began the retro park revolution in 1992, Pittsburgh's PNC Park perfected it nine years later. Located on the north bank of the Allegheny River between the Roberto Clemente and the Fort Duquesne bridges, the park was built to show off Pittsburgh, where baseball has been played since the days when steel was produced for locomotives, not automobiles. It was the Pirates fifth home

Located only blocks from where Three Rivers Stadium once stood, PNC Park is everything the old stadium wasn't—natural, intimate, and inviting. PNC is the first major-league park with just two decks to be built since Milwaukee County Stadium a half a century before it. As a result, it highest seat is just 88 feet from the field. Nearly three-quarters of the seats are on the field level. Fenway is the only major-league park with a smaller capacity.

Though many touches are borrowed from Forbes Field, where the Pirates played for 61 years, the view more resembles Exposition Park, which opened in 1882, and featured a view of barges floating down the Allegheny and Monongahela Rivers, not to mention smokestacks in the background.

The field dimensions are unique, with a nook in deep left that is 10 feet deeper than straight-away center. The outfield fences vary in height, ranging from just six feet in left field to 21 feet in right, honoring Clemente who wore No. 21.

The waters of the Allegheny are 443 feet, four inches from home plate, considerably further than McCovey Cove in San Francisco, but reachable on rare occasion by the game's most powerful left handed hitters. As in San Francisco, there is a walkway between the water and the park that gives fans views of the city and river, and a free look inside the park.

PNC Park relies on dark blue Pennsylvania steel, rather than the green more familiar in other new stadium. The distinctive light standards are modeled after those at Forbes Field.

Outside, a statue of Honus Wagner which first stood outside Forbes Field, and later Three Rivers, is at the home plate entrance. The Roberto Clemente statue was moved to the foot of his bridge, and a Willie Stargell statue greets visitors at the left field entrance. A statue for Bill Mazeroski was added at the right field entrance during the 2010 season—the 50th anniversary of the Pirates' 1960 World Series, which Mazeroski clinched with a Game 7 walk-off home run at Forbes Field.

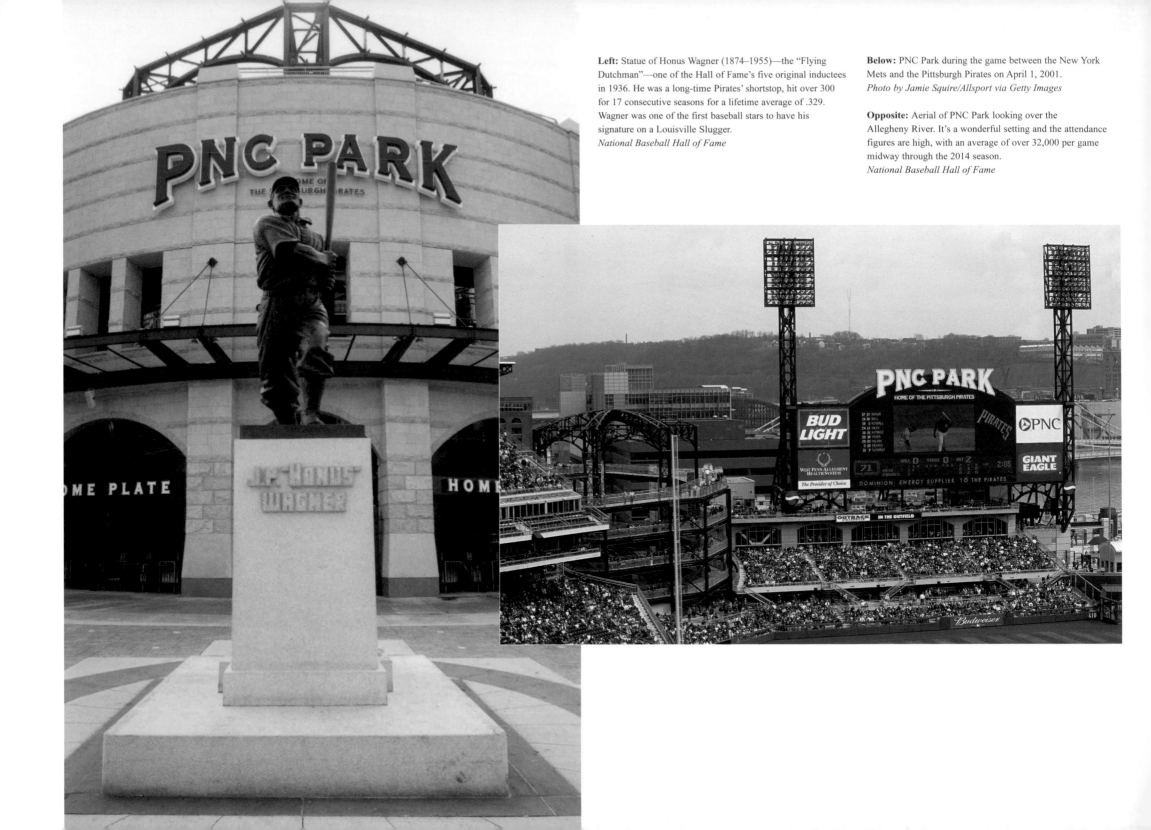

Left: Statue of Honus Wagner (1874–1955)—the "Flying Dutchman"—one of the Hall of Fame's five original inductees in 1936. He was a long-time Pirates' shortstop, hit over 300 for 17 consecutive seasons for a lifetime average of .329. Wagner was one of the first baseball stars to have his signature on a Louisville Slugger.
National Baseball Hall of Fame

Below: PNC Park during the game between the New York Mets and the Pittsburgh Pirates on April 1, 2001.
Photo by Jamie Squire/Allsport via Getty Images

Opposite: Aerial of PNC Park looking over the Allegheny River. It's a wonderful setting and the attendance figures are high, with an average of over 32,000 per game midway through the 2014 season.
National Baseball Hall of Fame

Left and Below: Three Rivers Stadium was knocked down on February 11, 2001. Built where the Allegheny, Monongahela, and Ohio Rivers come together, a cookie-cutter stadium resembling those in Philadelphia, Cincinnati, and St. Louis, Three Rivers was home to the Pirates as well as the NFL Steelers. *Time Life Pictures/Getty Images*

Left: On May 25, 1935, Babe Ruth hit the last home run of his major-league career in Forbes Field. The blast cleared the right-field wall, then cleared the screen and finally cleared the doubledeck grandstands. The historic shot (a first of that distance in Forbes Field) was approximately eighty-six feet high and at least three-hundred feet away from home plate.
National Baseball Hall of Fame

Right: View over the Forbes Field diamond. Known for its sheer size, the park was abandoned in favor of Three-Rivers Stadium, a cookie cutter park built at a cost of $40 million.
Time Life Pictures/Getty Images

FORBES FIELD (1909–70)

Forbes Field was among baseball's first luxury stadiums. Built beside one of the city's most upscale neighborhoods, it boasted elevators, electric lights, telephones, and even toilets for its patrons. The field was distinguished by its sheer size, which spread 376 feet to right field and 462 to dead center. The distance from home plate to the backstop was well over 100 feet, about double today's standard, frustrating generations of foul ball hitters.

The park was named after John Forbes, a general in the British Army who captured Fort Duquesne during the French and Indian War. Home to Honus Wagner, Ralph Kiner and Roberto Clemente, its most storied moment came in the bottom of the ninth inning during the final game of the World Series between the Pirates and the Yankees, when Bill Mazeroski hit a series ending ball high over the left-field wall. Part of the outfield wall remains on the University of Pittsburgh campus where the stadium once stood. The park was abandoned in 1970, in favor of ultra-modern, Three Rivers Stadium.

Right: Forbes Field was remarkably well-laid out, with landscaped gardens and statues
National Baseball Hall of Fame

FORBES FIELD
LAST OUT
6/28/70

Left: The last games at Forbes Field took place on June 28, 1970, as the Pirates played a doubleheader against the Cubs, their opponents in the first game ever at Forbes Field in 1909. The first game of the doubleheader saw the Pirates win 3–2. The second game, in front of 40,918, saw the Pirates end their stay at the ballpark with a final win, 4–1.
National Baseball Hall of Fame

ST. LOUIS CARDINALS

BUSCH STADIUM

ST. LOUIS CARDINALS

Address:
700 Clark Street
St. Louis, MO 63102
Capacity: 46,861
Opening day: April 10, 2006—St. Louis Cardinals 6, Milwaukee Brewers 4
Cost to construct: $400 million
Architect: HOK Sport (now Populous)
Dimensions (ft):
Left Field—336
Left Center—375
Center Field—400
Right Center—377
Right Field—335
Defining feature: Signature green fencing and red seats kept; statues from old stadium re-erected.
World Series: 2006, 2011
All-Star Game: 2009

Memorable moments:
2006 April 4—First game at the new stadium between two minor league Cardinals' affiliates: the Memphis Redbirds lose 5–3 to the Springfield Cardinals.
2006 October 7 and 8—First playoff game at the new stadium, Game 3 of the NLDS, sees the Padres defeat the Cardinals 3–1. The Redbirds win the next day's game and take the series 3–1.
2006 October 14—The Cardinals win the first of the NLCS games beating the Mets 5–0. They take the series 4–3.
2006 October 24, 26, and 27—Three World Series home games lead to three victories for the Cardinals over the Tigers and a 4–1 series triumph.
2011 October 19—The Cardinals win the first of the World Series against the Rangers.
2011 October 27—With the Rangers leading the series 3–2 one of the greatest games ever sees the Cardinals become the first team to come back from deficits in both the 9th and 10th innings. They win the game 10–9 and go on to win the next and the series.

When baseball elitists talk about a "cookie-cutter" stadium, they were talking about the old Busch Stadium built in 1966, opening just six months after the city's Gateway Arch on the banks of the Mississippi several blocks away. The Cardinals played their last game there on October 19, 2005, and moved into a new $400 million stadium—of course named Busch Stadium—for the 2006 season.

HOK Sport designed a retro-looking arena in brick and steel but were equally interested in paying tribute to the previous Busch Stadium. Statues from the latter were re-erected at various points around the new stadium—that of Cardinals' legend Stan Musial can be found outside the third base entrance, for example. The old stadium's scoreboard can be seen on the main concourse and the traditional green fencing and red seats have been maintained. Embedded in the exterior sidewalk are fan-purchased inscribed bricks that surround marble plaques celebrating 100 great moments in the Cardinals' history.

The Cardinals became one of baseball's glory teams between the mid-1920s and mid-1940s when they captured nine NL pennants—1926, 1928, 1930, 1931, 1934, 1942, 1943, 1944, and 1946—and six World Series titles. During the 1960s, they had three World Series teams—1964, 1967, and 1968—and they returned to the World Series three times in the 1980s

Since then, however, they advanced to the playoffs only once in the 1990s, losing the championship series to the Braves in 1996, and reached the World Series only once, in 2004, where they were swept by the Red Sox.

Imagine the joy, therefore, when the first season in the new Busch Stadium saw a home World Series victory—the first time this had happened since 1923.

With such a long and successful history, it is hardly surprising that many Cardinals have made it to the Hall of Fame—nineteen in total. Perhaps the franchise's greatest player of all time (or at least the one most connected with the team) was Stan "The Man" Musial, a Cardinal from 1941 to 1963. He won the Most Valuable Player award in 1943, 1946, and 1949, led the league in hitting seven times, and played in 21 All-Star games. So popular and influential a figure was Musial that a statue in his honor was unveiled outside the Busch Stadium in 1968; in 1969 he entered the Hall of Fame, in his first year of eligibility.

With dramatic views of the Gateway Arch and the downtown St. Louis skyline, a red brick exterior, expanded bleacher sections, a state-of-the art video board, and knowledgable fans, the new Busch Stadium is a great place to watch ball—and in recent seasons there have been some great games to watch: the 2009 All-Star Game; the 2011 World Series victory, including what some have called the greatest game in baseball history; 2012 postseason games against the Nationals and the Giants; and nine more in 2013. Spectator levels have been consistently high, topping three million, with the 2013 average of 41,602 the second best in the league.

Right: The interior of Busch Stadium during the third game at the ballpark, between the Brewers and the Cardinals, on April 13, 2006. The Brewers won 4–3 in the 11th in front of 40,222. *Elsa/Getty Images*

SPORTSMAN'S PARK (1902–66)

Home of the St. Louis Browns (AL) 1902-1953
Home of the St. Louis Cardinals (NL) 1920-1966

Baseball has been played on the corner of Grand and Dodier since 1871. It was in 1902 that Sportsman's Park was built, which boasts more major-league games than any park in history. For a remarkable 34 years, the stadium was home to both the Browns of the American League and the Cardinals of the National League. The two teams met in the 1944 World Series, with the Cardinals, the more dominant team during most of their joint history, coming out on top.

This is the park where Rogers Hornsby and Stan Musial played, where a goat in the 1940s helped the grounds crew keep the grass trim; where a midget was sent up by team owner Bill Veeck to draw a walk. It was also the last park in the majors to exclude African Americans from its general admission, providing them seats in the 1940s in a right field pavilion, which was screened so no home run balls could enter.

The Browns left for Baltimore in 1953, and the Cardinals moved into Busch Stadium after the 1966 season. The grandstands are gone, but baseball is still played on the field where Sportsman's once stood.

Left: Busch Stadium during the game between the St. Louis Cardinals and the Colorado Rockies on May 10, 2006. The Cardinals defeated the Colorado Rockies 7–4. The 630ft-tall Gateway Arch, opened in 1967, is a beautiful backdrop to the rather brighter illuminations within the ballpark. *Elsa/Getty Images*

Above: External view of Busch Stadium before Game Four of the 2006 World Series. *Dilip Vishwanat/Getty Images*

NATIONAL LEAGUE WEST

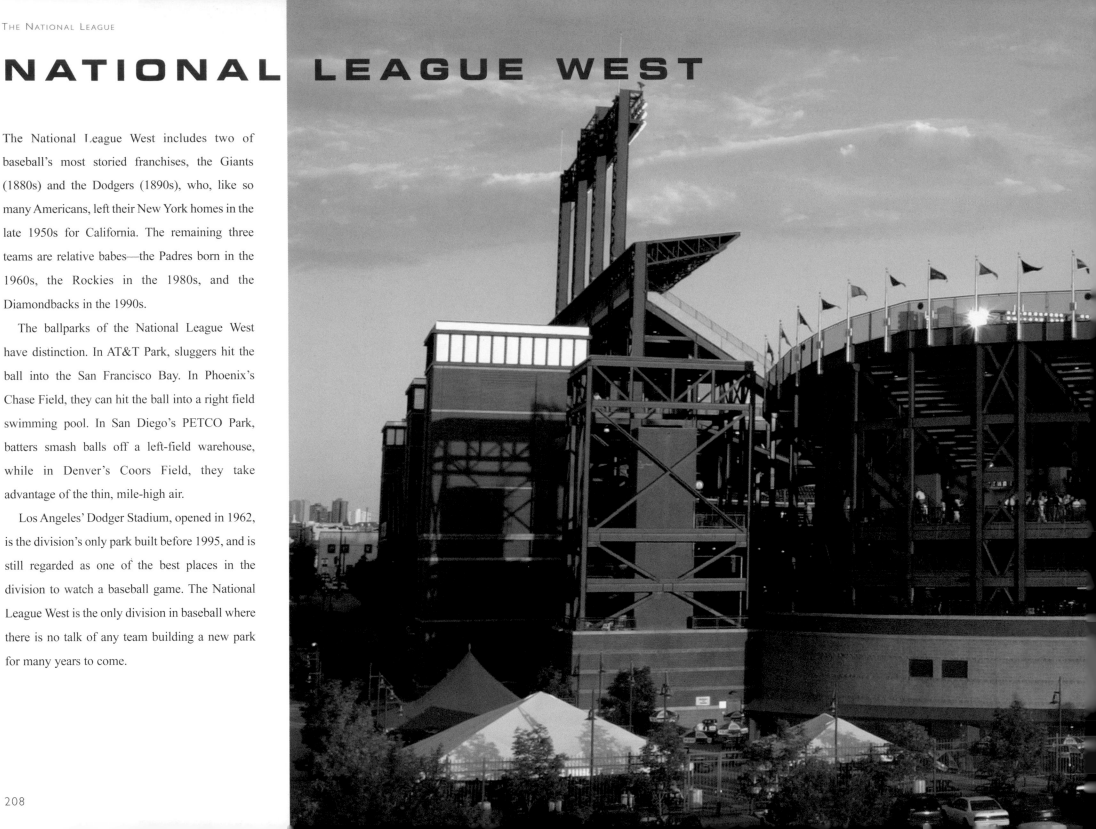

The National League West includes two of baseball's most storied franchises, the Giants (1880s) and the Dodgers (1890s), who, like so many Americans, left their New York homes in the late 1950s for California. The remaining three teams are relative babes—the Padres born in the 1960s, the Rockies in the 1980s, and the Diamondbacks in the 1990s.

The ballparks of the National League West have distinction. In AT&T Park, sluggers hit the ball into the San Francisco Bay. In Phoenix's Chase Field, they can hit the ball into a right field swimming pool. In San Diego's PETCO Park, batters smash balls off a left-field warehouse, while in Denver's Coors Field, they take advantage of the thin, mile-high air.

Los Angeles' Dodger Stadium, opened in 1962, is the division's only park built before 1995, and is still regarded as one of the best places in the division to watch a baseball game. The National League West is the only division in baseball where there is no talk of any team building a new park for many years to come.

Left: A general view of Coors Field prior to the National League game between the Arizona Diamondbacks and the Colorado Rockies on June 30, 2003. The Diamondbacks defeated the Rockies 8–7 in 12 innings.
Photo by Brian Bahr/Getty Images

ARIZONA DIAMONDBACKS
CHASE FIELD

ARIZONA DIAMONDBACKS

Aka: Bank One Ballpark
Address:
401 E. Jefferson Street
Phoenix, AZ 85004
Capacity: 49,033
Opening day: March 31, 1998—Colorado Rockies 9, Arizona Diamondbacks 2
Cost to construct: $354 million
Architect: Ellerbe Becket
Dimensions (ft):
Left Field—330
Left Center—374
Center Field—407
Right Center—374
Right Field—334
Defining feature: Right field swimming pool
World Series: 2001
All-Star Game: 2011

Memorable moments:
1999 July 11—Jay Bell hits a grand slam in the sixth inning, winning $1 million for fan Gylene Hoyle, who had predicted the player and the inning in a pre-game contest.
2001 May 8—Randy Johnson strikes out 20 Reds to tie a major-league record, yet does not record a win. The Diamondbacks ultimately triumph 4–3 in 11 innings.
2001 October 28—The Diamondbacks beat the Yankees 4–0 to take a two games to none lead in the World Series as Randy Johnson throws a three-hit, complete game shutout.
2001 November 4—Luis Gonzalez hits a bases-loaded single to score Jay Bell, capping a two-run, ninth-inning comeback to beat the Yankees 3–2 in the seventh game of the World Series.
2006 March—Chase Field hosts three first-round games of the World Baseball Classic.

Chase Field is a monument to the power of air conditioning.

The very qualities that make the Phoenix area such a popular destination for Cactus League games in the spring make it downright unbearable for baseball in the summer, when the average high temperature tops 100 degrees for three consecutive months.

Chase Field cools things down with 8,000 tons of air conditioning equipment, capable of creating enough cold air to chill 2,500 homes, and bring temperatures down by 30 degrees in three hours.

The unique retractable roof allows sunlight to shine on the natural turf, while keeping the oppressive desert heat from baking the grandstands. Nine million pounds of structural steel, using the same technology as a drawbridge, can open and close in less than five minutes, and can move into a variety of partially open positions.

With the climate under control, Chase Field can focus on baseball. More than 80 percent of the seats are located between the foul poles, and there is no upper deck in the outfield. Natural turf and an old-fashioned dirt path connecting the pitchers mound to home plate, give the park more of a classic feel than might be expected under a dome.

The stadium is cluttered with advertisements, among other distractions. Its most unique feature is the swimming pool and hot tub located just beyond the right field fence about 415 feet from home plate, where bathing suit clad patrons can buys tickets for a swim and a unique outfield view. Chicago's Mark Grace was the first to plunk a ball into the pool in May of 1998, a feat that has since been duplicated dozens of times.

Outside, Chase Field more resembles an airplane hanger than a baseball stadium. The red brick and green structural steel are said by the architects to blend into Phoenix's surrounding warehouse district, but the huge baseball murals on the side give it the look of a basketball or hockey arena.

Inside, the Diamondbacks boast a quarter mile of concession stands, and enough entertainment to draw 3.6 million fans its opening year. The park hosted the World Series in only its fourth year, beating the Yankees in a dramatic, come-from-behind, ninth-inning rally in game seven.

Originally named Bank One Ballpark, or as locals had it, the "BOB," after Bank One merged with J.P. Morgan Chase & Co., the name change was announced on September 23, 2005.

Right: External view of Chase Field in Phoenix.
Digitalballparks.com

Following page, Left: Front entrance of the then Bank One Ballpark. The $354 million cost of the structure was split between the Diamondback owners (32 percent) and public funding that came from a quarter-cent sales tax in Maricopa County.
Photo by Jeff Carlick /Allsport via Getty Images

Following page, Right: March 31, 1998: a view of batting practice before a game between the Diamondbacks and the Colorado Rockies. The Rockies defeated the Diamondbacks 9–2. The temperature is carefully controlled in the stadium, with the roof closed before games to allow the air conditioning to cool the interior. The architects also managed to allow a good quantity of natural light to filter through to the interior when the roof is closed, enough to play a daylight game without lights but without increasing the temperature. The opening roof also allows the field to be turfed.
Photo by Vincent Laforet /Allsport via Getty Images

Left: General Manager Jerry Colangelo of Arizona Diamondbacks throws the ceremonial first pitch before his team plays against the San Diego Padres during Opening Day at Bank One Ballpark April 1, 2002. The Diamondbacks won 2–0. *Photo by Donald Miralle/Getty Images*

Right: Chase Field boasts a 385 square-foot warm water pool and an 85 square-foot hot tub. *Digitalballparks.com*

COLORADO ROCKIES

COORS FIELD

COLORADO ROCKIES

Address:
2001 Blake Street
Denver, CO 80205
Capacity: 50,398
Opening day: April 26, 1995—Colorado Rockies 11, New York Mets 9 (14 innings)
Cost to construct: $215 million
Architect: HOK Sports
Dimensions (ft):
Left Field—347
Left Center—390
Center Field—415
Right Center—375
Right Field—350
Defining feature: Row of purple, mile-high seats
World Series: 2007
All-Star Game: 1998

Memorable moments:
1995 April 26—Dante Bichette christens the park with a 14th-inning, three-run home run, to beat the New York Mets 11–9 in the opening game.
1996 September 12—Ellis Burks steals his 30th base of the season, a month after hitting his 30th home run, to join baseball's elite 30–30 club. Teammate Dante Bichette joins him by hitting his 30th home run the following night.
1998 July 7—The American League beats the National League 13–8.
2001 September 9—Giants Barry Bonds hits home runs No. 61, 62, and 63 en route to his record 73-home run season.
2003 April 10—First baseman Todd Helton snags a line drive off the bat of Cardinal Orlando Palmeiro, setting in motion the Rockies first triple play.
2007 October 6—Rockies win 2–1 to sweep the Phillies and win the NLDS 3–0.
2007 October 15—Rockies win 6–4 to sweep Arizona and win the NLCS 4–0.
2007 October 28—Red Sox win the fourth game 4–3 and take the World Series.

The purple seats on the 20th row of Coors Field's upper deck tell the story of this ballpark. It is there that the elevation reaches 5,280 feet, exactly one mile above sea level. At that altitude balls fly further. Curve balls break less sharply. And that, more than any other feature, has defined the Rockies' home.

Coors Field, the first park in the National League to be constructed exclusively for baseball since Dodger Stadium 33 years earlier, is by no means a small park. Its center field fence is a deep 415 feet, and left center juts out nine feet deeper. Yet the dimensions are deceptive. According to a team estimate, a ball hit 400 feet at sea-level Yankee Stadium would travel 440 feet in mile high Coors Field. The thin air contributed to a record-setting 1999 season, when teams combined for an average of 15 runs and four home runs each game.

The incredible offense, the classic charm of the old-fashioned park, and the views of the Rocky Mountains in the distance, have made Coors Field among the best attended parks in baseball history.

The deep red brick and Colorado sandstone exterior makes Coors Field look like it has always been located in Denver's lower downtown, on a spot where a train depot once stood. The classic architecture and old fashioned corner front clock are reminiscent of Ebbets Field, and anchor a newly bustling downtown neighborhood.

Inside, the triple deck structure features small foul areas, an asymmetric field, and seats with sight lines geared toward the infield. A heating system under the field melts snow quickly, and its drainage system can clear away five inches of rain in a matter of hours.

The absence of an upper deck in left field provides fans along the first base and right field side a spectacular view of the Rocky Mountains. The stadium's designers passed up the chance to offer a panoramic view of downtown Denver so the sun would not be in batters' eyes, though the skyline is still visible from the top of the Rockpile, a 2,300-seat center field bleacher section where many tickets are held until game day, and kids and seniors can get in for just $1.

The park was originally designed to be even more intimate, seating just 43,000. But the huge popularity of baseball in nearby Mile High Stadium, where the Rockies played their first two years, persuaded the owners to add another 6,000 seats.

Right: Coors Field is a batter-friendly park and the height of the stadium above sea level is the reason. The air decreases in density the higher you are—the air is 15% less dense here than at most other, sea level, ballparks—so there are fewer air molecules to create friction against a flying baseball. This results in Coors Field sitting on top of the ESPN tables for "Park Factor"—which compares the rate of stats at home against those on the road. This doesn't mean the home team will necessarily win, of course, just that the stadium favors batters. This view of the baseball diamond is during the game between the St. Louis Cardinals and the Colorado Rockies on July 25, 1999. The Cardinals defeated the Rockies 10–6.
Photo by Brian Bahr/Allsport via Getty Images

Left: July 1998 photo of the Colorado Rockies playing the Pittsburgh Pirates.
Joseph Sohm; ChromoSohm Inc./Corbis

Left: A view toward the diamond and downtown Denver taken during a game between the Atlanta Braves and Colorado Rockies on June 18, 1995. A row of purple seats in the upper deck mark the elevation at exactly one mile above sea level.
Photo by Nathan Bilow/Allsport via Getty Images

Right: A view toward the Rocky Mountains: Coors Field has wonderful views from its substantial stands.
Photo by Jonathan Daniel/Allsport via Getty Images

LOS ANGELES DODGERS

DODGER STADIUM

LOS ANGELES DODGERS

Address:
1000 Elysian Park Avenue
Los Angeles, CA 90012
Capacity: 56,000 (reported: 53,400 is said to be more accurate)
Opening Day: April 10, 1962—Cincinnati Reds 6, Los Angeles Dodgers 3
Cost to construct: $23 million
Architect: Emil Praeger
Dimensions:
Left Field—330
Left Center—385
Center Field—395
Right Center—385
Right Field—330
Defining feature: Wavy roof over bleachers
Little-known ground rule: In its first year, the foul poles were mistakenly placed entirely in foul territory, and required special league dispensation to recognize balls that hit them as fair. Home plate was moved the following year to bring the poles into fair territory
World Series: 1963, 1965, 1966, 1974, 1977, 1978, 1981, 1988
All-Star Game: 1980

Memorable moments:
1963 October 6—The Dodgers sweep the Yankees in the World Series.
1968 June 4—Don Drysdale blanks Pittsburgh for his sixth consecutive shutout, a major-league record.
1969 August 5—Pirate Willie Stargell hits a home run completely out of Dodger Stadium, a feat he would accomplish twice. No one else has ever done it.
1981 April 27—Fernando Valenzuela blanks the Giants 5–0 for his fourth shutout in five starts, while posting an 0.20 ERA and a .438 batting average.
1988 October 15—Hobbling pinch hitter Kirk Gibson hits a two-strike, two-out, two-run homer off Oakland's Dennis Eckersley to win game one of the World Series 5 to 4.

Dodger Stadium isn't a "retro" park, nor does it pretend to be.

Five-tiered, perfectly symmetrical, and without a single deep red brick, Dodger Stadium sits atop Chavez Ravine as a testament to West Coast fans' affection for baseball.

At a time when old-fashioned, or neoclassical parks are the rage, Dodger Stadium stands out as the exception that proves there is more than one way to build a great baseball park.

For decades, what distinguished Dodger Stadium was its simplicity, its cleanliness, and its single-minded devotion to the game. Between the opening of Chicago's Wrigley Field in 1914 and Denver's Coors Field in 1995, Dodger Stadium was the only National League park built exclusively for baseball.

Dodger owner Walter O'Malley, who broke Brooklyn's heart by moving the Dodgers west, was given the site by the city of Los Angeles, which then evicted some disgruntled Mexican American residents from the hilltop, creating Latino animosity toward the Dodgers that persisted for decades.

The wayward Angels also played at Dodger Stadium until their park in Anaheim was opened in 1966, preferring to call it Chavez Ravine so as not to advertise their cross town rivals.

Deep power alleys have made this a pitchers' park, and Sandy Koufax, Don Drysdale, Fernando Valenzuala, and Orel Hershiser all thrived here. The grounds keeping is meticulous. More than 3,000 trees cover the 300-acre site, including several dozen trademark palm trees down the right and left field foul lines, which along with the Elysian Hills and the distant San Gabriel Mountains, give the park a distinctive Southern California look. The computer-controlled, Bermuda grass field, with state-of-the art vacuum chambers to assist draining, was rated No. 1 by baseball players in a *Sports Illustrated* survey in 2003.

The sight lines are on the mark, with no obstructed views. Each deck is freshly painted each season with its own color. Spectacular sunsets and the distinctive wavy roof over the bleachers give an instantly recognizable look to the stadium which was originally designed with the ability to expand to 85,000 seats, but has remained far smaller.

Dodger Stadium has hosted many events. Pope John Paul II celebrated mass there in 1987. The Beatles, the Rolling Stones, and the Three Tenors are among the long list of performers who have played on the field which also hosted Olympic baseball competition, the Harlem Globetrotters, boxing matches, and even a ski-jumping exhibition.

Over the past four decades the ballpark has been carefully improved. A video screen capable of showing instant replays, that debuted during the 1980 All-Star game, was baseball's first. Since 2000, the Dodgers have added new field level seats, and club suits, and a new state-of-the-art video screen. After the 2005 season all of the old seats were removed and replaced by new ones in yellow, light orange, turquoise, and sky blue. Ambitious plans to build a new Field Level concourse, with more concessions and restrooms, were completed in 2008.

In March 2012 Frank McCourt, owner since 2004, had to sell up to Guggenheim Baseball

Right: Dodger Stadium looks today much as it did when it opened in 1962. *National Baseball Hall of Fame*

Management for $2.15 billion thanks to a much publicized divorce. There was talk of moving the franchise but the new management put its money down not only to improve the team but also for major improvements to the structure under the direction of stadium specialist Janet Marie Smith.

The effect on the team was immediate: the Dodgers won the Western Division title in 2013. The stadium also improved: for 2013 there were new HD hexagonal video boards, a new sound system, wider concourses, and more standing room viewing areas. For 2014, the investment of $150 million saw expansion of the entries at the field level, two new 25,000 square-foot plazas in right and left field; viewing areas overlooking the bullpens; a new walkway allowing fans on field level to do a 360 degree interior walk; a new state of the art wireless system throughout; enhancement of the ballpark's landscaping—the Three Sisters are back beyond the bullpen and more than 90 new trees are part of the new plaza area—and improved vehicular and pedestrian access.

Right: Another sellout crowd enjoys a game at Dodger Stadium. In recent years the Dodgers have continued to enjoy high attendances: in 2012 the stadium was the fifth best in MLB, ESPN reporting a season total of 3,324,246. In 2013 Dodger Stadium was at the top with an attendance total of 3,743,527—over 46,000 a game. Their remarkable comeback—from bottom of the division on June 21 to winners on September 19—may have helped, of course! *Photo by: Robert Landau/ Corbis*

Right: External view of the stadium, showing some of the 3,400 trees planted in the 300-acre site. Dodger Stadium has parking facilities for 16,000 automobiles.
Digitalballparks.com

Far Right: The classic lines of Ebbets Field seen during the 1956 World Series.
National Baseball Hall of Fame

EBBETS FIELD
(1913–57)
Home of the Brooklyn Dodgers

Ebbets Field is arguably where baseball became the national pastime. For 45 years, the stadium between Brooklyn's Bedford and Flatbush neighborhoods defined what it meant to go the ballpark. From its brick arched exterior to its ornate domed rotunda, many of today's stadiums reflect its memory. Seats were close to the field. The outfield wall framed a uniquely shaped field. Its trademark Shaefer Beer billboard flashed an "H" for hits and an "E" for errors. Clothier Abe Stark invited players to hit his advertisement on the outfield fence for a free suit, something he never needed to pay up.

It was here that Jackie Robinson broke the color barrier in 1947, where television broadcast its first game, where the Dodgers won nine pennants, and where owner Walter O'Malley broke Brooklyn's heart by taking his team to Los Angeles.

In its final years, O'Malley complained that the stadium was falling apart, and he searched for a new home. He was not satisfied with the plot of land offered to him in Queens where the Mets would end up several years later. He left Brooklyn for the west after the 1957 season. The wrecking balls began demolishing the park in 1960. Today, the site is home to a low-income housing project, aptly named the Jackie Robinson apartments.

Left: Opening day for Brooklyn Stadium—that would become Ebbets Field. Rival teams line the diamond as the band plays and a procession nears the home plate where it will sing the national anthem. *Digitalballparks.com*

Right: The Dodgers played their last game at Ebbets Field on September 24, 1947, before moving to the west coast. The stadium was demolished in 1960.

SAN DIEGO PADRES

PETCO PARK

SAN DIEGO PADRES

Address:
100 Park Boulevard, San Diego
CA 92173
Capacity: 42,302
Opening day: April 8, 2004. San Diego Padres 4, San Francisco Giants 3 (10 innings)
Cost to construct: $449 million
Architect: HOK Sports
Dimensions (ft):
Left Field—336
Left Center—383
Center Field—396
Right Center—392
Right Field—322
Defining feature: Left field Western Metal Supply Co. Buildin. When the Padres hit a home run a foghorn is sounded.
World Series: None
All-Star Game: 2006

Memorable moments:

2004 March 11—first game at the park saw the San Diego State Aztecs defeat Houston.
2004 April 15—Mark Loretta hits the Padres' first home run at the stadium.
2005 November 11—The Rolling Stones play a concert at the stadium. Madonna performs there in 2008.
2006 March 18 and 20—the semi-finals and finals of the first World Baseball Classic are played at PETCO. Japan wins the inaugural tournament.
2007 August 4—Barry Bonds hits his 755th homer, tying with Hank Aaron
2008 April 17—The Padres and Rockies play a 22-innings game, which the Rockies win 2–1.
2010 May 31—The Padres beat the Mets 18–6.
2010 June 14—Earthquake stops play briefly in the 8th.
2011 April 8—Rain stops play three times and the game against the Dodgers is finished the next day.

Baseball was played in downtown San Diego before there really was a downtown. More than a 130 years later, the bustling city center is home to a much-admired downtown stadium, just blocks from the spot of the first sandlot games.

Petco Park is a "retro" stadium with a distinctly Southern California look. Surrounded by jacaranda trees, water walls, natural stone, and a stucco exterior, the park offers panoramic views of downtown skyscrapers, Mission Bay, Balboa Park, and the arid mountains that surround the city.

Its trademark feature is a left-field warehouse, the turn-of-the-century Western Metal Supply Co. building. Though far smaller than Camden Yard's B&O warehouse, it directly abuts the field, creating an irresistible target for right handed hitters. The left corner of the building holds the left-field foul pole, and each of its four floors contains outdoors seating and a unique perspective on the game.

Unlike the Padres' old home at Qualcomm Stadium, also known as Jack Murphy Field, Petco Park was built exclusively for baseball. The park is intimate, with 20,000 fewer seats than Qualcomm, three decks rather than four, seats located much closer to the field, and all angled toward the pitchers mound. The park boasts a capacity of 46,000, though there are only 42,000 seats, reflecting a range of standing room options for fans who can see the ballgame from the concourse and a variety of porches and terraces, in addition to the center field "Park at the Park," a grass park and picnic area for about 2,500 fans.

The unusual (and much ridiculed) name comes from the San Diego-based retailer of pet supplies, which bought the naming rights reportedly for $60 million over 22 years.

Outside, where the early sandlot games were played, the ballpark is anchor to a larger downtown redevelopment project, with plans for a new library, museum, and apartments. Immediately outside the stadium are two noteworthy features. First there is the Palm Court Plaza, the main entrance from the Gaslamp District. This consists of a grid-like pattern of bricks, each placed in a quadrant named after a baseball term and bearing a message from fans. There is also the Park in the Park, an area directly behind the center field area. This contains a Little League infield, Picnic Hill, and a statue of the legendary Tony Gwynn surrounded by 2,000 bricks, again inscribed with fans' messages.

The pitcher-friendly confines of Petco were altered after the 2012 season. The center field walls were moved in (left from 402 to 390 feet, right from 402 feet to 391 feet), and the right field wall from 360 to 349 feet. (It was also lowered to eight feet.) On top of this, the visiting team bullpen was moved from foul territory in right field to behind the Padres' bullpen. The changes didn't make the ballpark qualify as neutral, but improved batting chances at a franchise that has ranked last in the Major Leagues in runs scored at home four times since opening (2006–2009) and 29th on two occasions (2005, 2011).

Right: The San Diego Padres play against the New York Mets at Petco Park on April 30, 2004.
© *David Madison/NewSport/Corbis*

Left: The exterior of Petco Park, March 13, 2013, looking towards the Home Plate Gate.
Bernard Gagnon via wikicommons

Right: Petco is an attractive, intimate ballpark with breathtaking views over San Diego.
abrowncoat via wikicommons

Following pages: Two views of Qualcomm Stadium with scoreboard detail. 2003 was the final season for the Padres in Qualcomm Stadium. Constructed in 1967, "the Q" had been the Padres' home since their inaugural season in 1969. It hosted a pair of World Series (1984 and 1998) and a pair of Major League Baseball All-Star games (1978 and 1992).
Digitalballparks.com

Far Left: Night view of Qualcomm from above first base. *Digitalballparks.com*

Left: Qualcomm's capacity was 67,544 in 1997. *Digitalballparks.com*

Below, Inset: Opening day national anthem before the April 1, 1997, game between the New York Mets and San Diego. The Padres won the game 12–5. *Photo by Jed Jacobsohn/Allsport via Getty Images*

SAN FRANCISCO GIANTS

AT&T PARK

SAN FRANCISCO GIANTS

Aka: Pac Bell Park (2000–03), SBC Park (2003–05)
Address:
801 Third Street
San Francisco, CA 94107
Capacity: 41,915
Opening day: April 11, 2000—Los Angeles Dodger 6, San Francisco Giants 5
Cost to construct: $319 million
Architect: HOK Sports
Dimensions (ft):
Left Field—335
Left Center—364
Center Field—404
Right Center—420
Right Field—307
Defining feature: McCovey Cove
Most expensive seat: $75
Cheapest seat: $10
World Series: 2002, 2010, 2012
All-Star Game: 2007

Memorable Moments:
2000 May 1—Barry Bonds hits the first regulation game ball into McCovey Cove, a seventh-inning shot off Rich Rodriguez of the NY Mets.
2002 August 9—Bonds joins Hank Aaron, Babe Ruth, and Willie Mays as the only players to hit 600 HRs.
2002 October 14—Kenny Lofton hits a two-out, ninth-inning single to beat the St. Louis Cardinals 2–1 and send the Giants to their first World Series since 1962: they lose to the Angels.
2010 October 28—Nate Schierholtz makes a running catch to end the second World Series game against the Rangers 9–0. Three days later the Giants win their first World Series since 1954.
2012 October 25—A shutout win in Game 2 of the World Series gives the Giants a 2–0 lead over the Tigers. Two more wins in Detroit and the title returns to San Francisco.

Ask any five-year old. There is a primal satisfaction that comes from splashing a solid object into a body of water.

The Giants have taken this proposition to major-league heights at SBC Park, where the chilly waters of the San Francisco Bay sit a tantalizing 352 feet from home plate.

There is much that is appealing about the Giants' new home. The park is small and its dimensions intimate. The sight lines are engineered exclusively for baseball. The field is asymmetrical with a 25-foot high brick wall just 309 feet from home plate, the closest foul pole in the majors. The view beyond the outfield is as beautiful an urban landscape as can be imagined.

But for all its charms, nothing compares to the childishly irresistible anticipation that a powerful left handed hitter might clear the 25-foot brick wall in right field, and plop a home run into the water named after the Giants' Hall of Fame first baseman Willie McCovey. The Giants have such a hitter, and SBC is unmistakably the park that (Barry) Bonds built. Just as the Yankees erected a short right-field fence in 1923

for their star left hander, Babe Ruth, the Giants built SBC for Bonds, the marquee power hitter of his time. As the 2004 season opened, only four players had "gone Bay," but Bonds himself has done it 27 times, thrilling capacity crowds who were just warming up after four decades at frigid Candlestick Park.

Just as fans gather on Chicago's Waveland Avenue for the chance at a home run ball, sailors, kayakers, and other boaters fill McCovey Cove during Giants games, their eyes fixed on the right field fence. The location is so close that when the Yankees Jorge Posada hit the ball into the cove during an exhibition game, the ball was scooped up by boater Mike Quinby who promptly threw it back onto the field on a fly.

SBC was built in the mold of Camden Yards. Rather than the B&O warehouse in right field, it is the Bay, with stunning vistas of the East Bay hills and the Bay Bridge from the upper deck. Architects resisted even more sweeping views in order to reduce the wind, and to give Bonds a better shot at reaching the Bay. Temperatures are not nearly as cold as at windy Candlestick,

where former Giants pitcher Stu Miller was famously blown off the mound during the 1961 All-Star Game. Still, you won't catch many locals wearing short sleeves at night.

The inside is bustling with activity, from an 80-foot long Coca Cola bottle in left field, which houses slides for kids, and a 27-foot baseball glove at its spout, to a miniature SBC park, where kids can smack Wiffle balls over the fence. Outside, a statue of Willie Mays is a central meeting spot near the park's main entrance, and another of McCovey overlooks his cove on the Bay side.

Known as Pac Bell Park when it opened, the name changed in 2004 after Texas-based communications company SBC (Southwest Bell Corp.) bought the local phone company, putting some San Franciscans in the awkward position of clamoring for the park's original corporate name. SBC is the first privately financed park in Major League Baseball since Dodger Stadium in 1962.

When SBC merged with AT&T Corp. in 2005 the park's name changed again.

Pac Bell (now AT&T) Park: note the Coke bottle (see page 245) and the park's waterside position.

Right: Aerial View of SBC Park. While there have been plenty of balls hit into the water, ESPN rates AT&T Park as the most pitcher-friendly ballpark in the National League—mainly due to the depth of the outfield. This hasn't affected attendance. Helped by their success, in recent years fan numbers have been excellent: in 2011 the total was 3,387,303 (third in MLB), in World Series-winning 2012 the total was 3,387,303 (fourth), and they were third again in 2013 with 3,377,371. This is all part of a long sell-out streak that, on April 27, 2014, with the 258th consecutive sellout, established a record in National League history. MLB.com reported their last last non-sellout at home was September 30, 2010, against Arizona. The Boston Red Sox have the all-time record: 794 home sellouts at Fenway Park from May 15, 2003, to April 8, 2013.
Photo by Douglas Peebles/Corbis

Above Left: Viewed from one of the luxury boxes at SBC Park is McCovey Cove, a splash target for left-handed sluggers throughout the league. The Cove is separated from the right field seats by a promenade, popular with casual fans interested in catching a play or two while passing by on a summer's walk.
*Photo by Deanne Fitzmaurice/*San Francisco Chronicle

Left: Giants fans fill up McCovey Cove in all manner of water craft whenever slugger Barry Bonds steps up to the plate. Each hopes to catch or at least retrieve a home run souvenir from a game at SBC Park , until the 2004 season, known as Pacific Bell Park. A Bonds at bat is definitely the best chance of doing so. Of the 31 "splash hits" since the park opened in 2001, Barry Bonds has hit 27.
*Photo by Carlos Avila Gonzalez/*San Francisco Chronicle

Above: The great Giants' slugger, Barry Bonds, walking to the on deck Circle before his first at bat in a game at Pac Bell Park on September 13, 2003.
*Photo by Liz Mangelsdorf/*San Francisco Chronicle

Right: General view of SBC Park during the national anthem before game three of the National League championship series between the Cardinals and the Giants on October 12, 2002.
Photo by Matthew Stockman /Getty Images

Left: Stand-in Pitcher Kirk Rueter—#46 of the San Francisco Giants—throws a pitch during game five of the National League Championship series against the St. Louis Cardinals on October 14, 2002. The Giants won the game 2–1 and the series 4–1. Behind him are the left field bleachers and, above them, the Coca-Cola Fan Lot and Giant 1927 Old-Time Four-Fingered Baseball Glove. The Coke bottle is 80-feet long, contains viewing platforms and four slides—two 56-foot-long curving slides (the "Guzzler") and two 20-foot-long twisting slides (the "Twist-Off"). The baseball mitt is 26-feet-high, 32-feet-wide and 12-feet-deep and made of steel and fiberglass.
Getty Images

Far Left: Fans stand in a moment of silence in a pre-game ceremony in honor of the victims of September 11 before the game between the Dodgers and the Giants at Pacific Bell Park on September 11, 2002. The Dodgers defeated the Giants 7–3.
Getty Images

Right: In recognition of the Hall of Fame player who wore the Giants' #24 for twenty-two seasons, this nine-foot bronze statue of the great Willie Mays welcomes fans to the entrance to the newly renamed SBC Park at 24 Willie Mays Plaza. The 24 palm trees that line the plaza are another part of the tribute to one of baseball's most honored and beloved players.
*Photo by Scott Sommerdorf/*San Francisco Chronicle

Inset, Right: At 5:04 on October 17, 1989, a 7.1 earthquake struck the San Francisco Bay Area as the Giants and Oakland A's were preparing for game three of that year's World Series. This photo shows the scene at Candlestick Park moments after the quake hit, rattling the press boxes, knocking out power, and prompting a giant roar from the shaken fans. The game was postponed minutes later. The A's went on to sweep the Giants in four games.
*Photo by John O'Hara/*San Francisco Chronicle

Left: September 30, 1999: A general view of the last game at 3 Com Park, commonly known as Candlestick Park, between the Dodgers and the Giants. The Dodgers defeated the Giants 9–4. Having moved to San Francisco from the New York Polo Grounds (see pages 244–245) in 1958, the Giants played their games at Seals Stadium while they waited for their new home to be constructed. It was ready for April 12, 1960, when the then Vice President, Richard Nixon, threw the first ball. The stadium played host to many significant events: The Beatles played here in August 1966 (their last full concert); there were two All-Star Games (1961 and 1984; and, of course, two Wolrd Series, that of 1962 (lost to the Yankees) and the 1989 "Battle of the Bay", which was so famously interrupted by an earthquake (see inset photo opposite) and won by Oakland.
Jed Jacobsohn/Allsport via Getty Images

Left: Exterior view of Candlestick park as boats bring fans in for opening day game against St. Louis Cardinals, April 12, 1960. The vast parking lot had space for around 10,000 vehicles when built.
Photo by Jon Brenneis/Time Life Pictures/Getty Images

Far Left: The interior of the Stick changed considerably in the winter of 1970–1971 when it was enclosed, as part of the deal that brought the NFL San Francisco 49ers to share the stadium. The most immediate changes, other than the increase in seating, were the loss of the view of the bay and a marginal improvement on the windiness.
Photo by Otto Greule Jr/Getty Images

Left and Far Left: Not all fans remember Candlestick Park as being a great ballpark—"a terrible place to get to, a freezing place to watch a game" sums up the general view. The breeze off the bay meant that even in July spectators would bring blankets to keep themselves warm ... in California! Marginally better when enclosed, the stadium saw an increase in seating from 45,000 to 61,000 and some great NFL action during its 1971–2013 tenure by the 49ers: eight NFC Championship games were played there.
National Baseball Hall of Fame

This Page: Views of the Polo Grounds.
National Baseball Hall of Fame

This Page: The New York Giants left the Polo Grounds in 1957, having played in various incarnations of the stadium since 1883. They won five World Series and seventeen National League pennants from the Polo Grounds. The Giants moved to the West Coast at the same time as the Brooklyn Dodgers moved to Los Angeles. Two dissenting voices on the Giants' board—Joan Payson and M. Donald Grant—would go on to found the Mets in 1962. Here, various views of the Polo Grounds.
Associated Press/National Baseball Hall of Fame; Corbis/National Baseball Hall of Fame

Following Page: An aerial view of SBC Park, then known as Pacific Bell Park, framed by the San Francisco skyline as fans arrive about an hour before the first pitch the park's first game ever, an exhibition between the Giants and the Milwaukee Brewers in March of 2000.
Brant Ward/San Francisco Chronicle

INDEX